AN OLD COUNTRY GIRL'S GIRL'S BEGINNING

My First 90 Years – Book 1

Bonnie Lacey Krenning

For information regarding permission, write to:
Starla Enterprises, Inc.
Attention: Permissions Department,
9415 E. Harry St., Ste. 603, Wichita, KS 67207

First Edition

ISBN: 9798551631194

Edited by Starla Criser

Cover Design by Sharon Revell

Printed in the U.S.A.

DEDICATION

This story collection of my memories is dedicated to my beloved husband, William "Bill" John Krenning.

About Bonnie Lacey Krenning

After nearly nine decades of living, Bonnie is still going strong. She has led a challenging life and continues to treasure each day given to her.

Her husband, Bill, was her soulmate for fifty-eight years before he passed. Their family of four grown children, seven grandchildren, ten great-grandchildren, and two great-great-grandchildren are of key importance in her life.

Throughout her life, she has had many helpful pleasures, including sewing, gardening, and redecorating. Her dream of being a nurse since age six became a reality at age forty-eight.

Upon that graduation, Bill bought her a Cessna 150 as a special gift. Not long after that, at age fifty, she had the chance to fulfill another of her dreams, that of being a pilot.

In their many years together, Bonnie and Bill had the opportunity to vacation throughout the United States. And Bonnie had the chance to go on mission trips to Ephesus and China. Bill declined those trips, claiming he had gone on enough "missions" during his time in the military service.

TABLE OF CONTENTS

HE PICKED ME UP
OFF THE STREET

One day our daughter Susan asked, "Dad, how did you and Mom meet?"

Bill set his elbows on the table before him, cleared his throat, and in a mock, low tone said, "I picked her up off the street."

We were celebrating his 75th birthday with our grown children. They filmed him talking about his childhood, time in the military during the war, and our early years together. After his teasing statement, they filmed him, elaborating in great detail about how we met. We still have it in a treasured film.

The following is my telling of how we met and eventually became a couple.

On a Sunday morning, March 15th, at church, a girlfriend told me about some guys she met the night before at the skating rink. They wanted to meet some girls. I told her I wasn't interested. I had never dated because I didn't want to date.

That afternoon, a beautiful day, I walked the mile to church for Easter choir practice. A 1931 Model A Ford pulled up beside me and stopped. I turned and saw two guys and my girlfriend in the back seat of the car.

The driver opened the passenger door and asked me where I was going. I noticed he was handsome, with bright blue eyes and dimples as he smiled.

When I told him, he said, "If you want to get in, I'll take you there."

Since my girlfriend was in the car and it was broad daylight, I took the offer and climbed into the passenger seat. He said his name was Bill, I told him my name, and he drove us to the church.

We got to church early, so we walked to a park close by and took pictures. So, I have photos of the day we met. Before I left for choir practice, Bill asked me to go with him to a movie that night. I told him I was going to church and invited him to go with me, and he agreed. Then, telling him where I lived, I went to choir practice.

After choir practice, I walked home, excited and thinking about my first date. When I got home, I told Mom a boy was coming to take me to church that evening.

She looked surprised, and then asked, "What is his name?"

I said, "Bill."

"Bill who?"

"I don't remember." He had told me his last name, but I forgot it.

She asked, "Where is he from?"

"I don't know."

If the date hadn't been going to church, I don't know whether she would have let me go. Especially if she had known that Bill was twenty-two years old and a veteran of World War II. I didn't know that either, until a few days later.

My family knew I hadn't been interested in dating. They thought I would be an old maid. Surprised and curious, they all gathered around in the living room that evening, waiting for Bill to come to the door.

As he walked up the porch steps, I invited him into the living room. Turning around, I saw Daddy sitting in his easy chair across the room. My sister and five brothers, some sitting and some standing, lined up around the room. Mom was standing in the doorway to the kitchen. I introduced Bill to them, and then we left quickly to go to church.

If William "Bill" John Krenning could have been scared away, it surely would have been that evening. But he "Doesn't scare easy," as the old saying goes. We went to church together. It was our first date, my first date.

So, I guess in a way he did pick me up off the street.

Bill and Bonnie on left side, 1947

GRANDMA STROER'S LEGACY

I remember Grandma Stroer being the size of us kids when I was five or six years old. Maggie Barnard Stroer was four feet ten inches tall and weighed about ninety pounds. According to her church, she believed that women should not show their "limbs," she didn't say arms or legs. She wore long sleeves to her wrists and dresses to cover her high-top, lace-up shoes. She wore one-and-a-half-inch heels, which helped her height some. She never went outside in the daytime without her sunbonnet to cover her long, light brown hair, which had never been cut.

In contrast, Grandpa was a large, heavy-set man, twice Grandma's size. William (Billie) Stroer wore denim overalls and a blue chambray shirt. I never saw him wear anything else.

Grandma Stroer was born in Virginia in 1879, but her family homesteaded in Kansas when she was a small child. The family didn't like the Kansas wind and cold winter, so her father moved them to Cedar County, Missouri, after a year.

Grandpa was born in Pawnee County, Kansas, in 1877. His family moved to Cedar County, Missouri, when he was a child, too.

Maggie was an unmarried sixteen-year-old girl when she had her first child on December 26, 1896, in Cedar County. Soon after the birth, she married the young man she had been dating. As Anna Mae Stroer grew up, her mother told her Billie was not her father. She always adored her "Poppy," loving and respecting him, even more when she did learn as an adolescent that he had willingly become her "Father."

Having a baby when not married was a scandal and a disgrace. Marrying an unwed mother was also considered a disgrace. The custom was that nobody saw a mother-to-be in public after they were "showing." So, they may have been able to keep the community from knowing she just had a baby since she was living in a remote area.

My aunt Elizabeth, their youngest daughter, was sixteen when I was six years old. She persuaded Mom to let me stay with them in town for a week. She worked at the drug store, and sometimes she and I walked the few blocks there to get me an ice cream cone. She introduced me to her many friends. I was shy, but I loved all the attention that I had never had before.

During the week, Grandma took me to town in the evening to hear the high school band practice in the park's pavilion. We visited with her friends, who all called her "Grandma." Grandpa had retired from farming, and when he wasn't gardening, he spent most of his time sitting in his rocking chair on the front porch during the day and in the evening.

One evening I was sitting on a chair beside him. Grandma came out to tell him supper was ready. She did something I had never seen grown-ups, especially "old people," do. Standing beside him, she put her arms around him and kissed him for what I thought was no reason at all. They seemed so happy, and both smiled. That moment was one of my most pleasant memories.

Being pampered for a week was so special. The visit to Grandma's and Grandpa's house was so much fun. When I got back home, I just wanted to play and do nothing, but Mom stopped that. She soon had me back in my routine, drying the dishes and setting the table, among other chores.

When my family moved from the farm to Joplin and other places, we didn't see Grandma and Grandpa so much. One summer after the war started, my brother, Jesse, came home on leave before going overseas into combat. He wanted to see Grandma before he left. Jesse, his wife, Bonnie, Mom, and I drove from Winchester, Kansas to El Dorado Springs to visit Grandma.

El Dorado Springs is built on sloping hillsides. Grandma's lawn sloped down to the sidewalk with a two-foot drop with a retaining wall at the edge. As we drove up by her house and got out of the car, we saw her standing in the doorway. She grabbed her long skirts, ran down the steps, dashed across the lawn, jumped down onto the sidewalk, and grabbed Jesse in a big hug. She was in her sixties then.

Grandpa was always in the background but was always there. Until…

When I had just turned fourteen, we got a phone call that Grandpa had died of a heart attack. My family immediately drove to El Dorado Springs. I was shocked at what I saw and heard! It was customary to prepare the body for burial, place it in the coffin, and keep the body at their house until the funeral. When someone came to visit, they opened the coffin, and they mourned and cried with Grandma. She didn't hold back. One of the men kept watch over the coffin at night, and I would hear Grandma softly sobbing in the night by the coffin. We didn't get much sleep for several nights.

The whole funeral ordeal was a lot for a fourteen-year-old girl to experience. It started with the slow, twenty-mile funeral procession drive to the cemetery, where a crowd of people waited. The graveside service was lovely with singing and a sermon. Grandpa was much loved and respected by many, especially me.

For the rest of her life, Granma had sons or her daughter living with her, or she lived with them. In the early 1950s, Grandma became "liberated." Her church was relaxing their rules. She started wearing dress shoes, short sleeves, her skirts at mid-calf, and no more sunbonnets. She had her long hair cut for the first time in her life and had it permed.

After Bill and I married in 1949, we only saw Grandma once or twice a year for several years. In 1960 we moved to Wichita, where Mom and most of my family lived. Grandma's sons and daughters brought her from Kansas City to Wichita often, especially to see Mom.

When Mom was in her late sixties, she developed Parkinson's Disease and what the doctor called "Crippling Arthritis." She was in a wheelchair and required more care than we could provide in our home, so she moved to a nursing home. We brought her to our family gatherings, which was most weekends.

One weekend in mid-August, Mom's brother and his wife brought Grandma from Kansas City to visit Mom. It was Grandma's birthday. We gathered at my brother's home for a big birthday dinner for her. After dinner, she brought two large, ripe peaches and gave them to Mom.

Grandma's daughter-in-law told this story:

"Early this morning, when we were getting ready to leave, I couldn't find Mom (Grandma). I looked out the window, and she was climbing in the peach tree. I ran out and asked her what she was doing, climbing a tree. She calmly said, 'I have been watching for those peaches to fall so I could take them to Annie Mae. When they didn't fall, I had to climb the tree and get them.'" Grandma was in her mid-eighties.

Mom departed this life over ten years before Grandma did. Grandma attended the funeral. She did some loud mourning and crying at the service like most of us had never heard. Some of us may have wished to express feelings more fully as Grandma did but were reluctant to do so, especially me.

When Grandma was in her mid-eighties, she lived with her daughter in a small town near Kansas City. She was still as busy as ever gardening in the summertime as she had all her life. She walked about in the small town, doing errands for her friends. The post office didn't deliver the mail. You had to pick it up there. Grandma picked up mail for her older, sometimes younger, friends that were not as able as she was.

One summer, they hospitalized Grandma for heart problems, and I went to visit her. She was annoyed and told me, "I want to go home so I can get the mail for my friends because they depend on me." They dismissed her in a few days

We had a ninetieth birthday party for Grandma. Hundreds of people attended, both family and friends. Throughout the day, some of us tried to count Grandma's direct descendants. We stopped counting when we reached over two hundred grandchildren, great-grandchildren, and great-great-grandchildren. There were five generations, maybe six. She enjoyed her family and spent most of her time caring for her grandchildren because that was what she wanted to do.

In her mid-nineties, her health began to fail. They admitted her to the hospital with heart failure. I got a call from my aunt Elizabeth that Grandma wasn't eating in the hospital and was losing weight. I drove to Kansas City to stay with her for a few days. She was weak and in bed. I had never seen her so frail. The nurse said she only weighed sixty pounds and was now just four feet, six inches tall. I was pretty strong then, and when she wanted to go to the bathroom, I picked her up and carried her there.

Grandma wasn't checking her menu for the foods she wanted because she had never learned to read. When I asked her why she wasn't eating, she said, "These victuals here ain't fit to eat. Why, they don't even fry their fish!" Without Grandma knowing, I told the nurse that she couldn't read. The staff started reading the menu to her and allowed her to choose anything she wanted. She began to gain weight, and after several days they dismissed her from the hospital. I don't think she would ever have told them that she couldn't read and may have died as a result.

While I was there several days with her in the hospital, we talked about old times. I wondered if I could get her to say anything about Mom's birth and her being born before Grandma was married. I said, "Grandma, tell me about Mom when she was born, and when she was a baby."

Grandma was leaning back in the recliner. She sat up straight and said, "My oldest married sister wanted to buy my baby! I told her there wasn't a room big enough to hold enough money to buy my baby!" It became obvious to me that she wasn't going to say anything more about that subject, so we changed the conversation.

It was common when Mom was born to sell a baby to a relative under those circumstances. I'm so thankful that Grandma did not sell Mom. If she had sold Mom to her sister, I would never have been "me." Or maybe Grandma would then have become my "great aunt." Who knows?

A couple of years later, at ninety-six years of age, Grandma moved on to Heaven to be with her beloved Billie and her Jesus. She left a legacy of perseverance, endurance, contentment, and joy that I shall always cherish.

William and Maggie Stroer with sons, 1940s

Maggie Stroer in her 70s

SUCH IS MY BEGINNING

I have relied on what my seven older brothers, Mom, and Daddy told me about when I was born and my early years of life. They say, and the records show, that I was born on March 2, 1931. We lived on a rented farm in Cedar County, Missouri, then a remote part of the state. There was no electricity or indoor plumbing for miles around, even in the schools, churches, and the country store. Few people had cars.

I recall one afternoon in October when I was four and a half years old. Daddy was at the house and told my brothers and me to stay outside and play because Mom wasn't feeling well. She was in bed. As we were playing, I looked up and saw a man in a suit walking up the hill toward the house. He had left his car at the bottom of the hill because the bridge was out over the creek. He was carrying a black bag. My brothers told me that doctors bring babies in a black bag. No one told me Mom was getting another baby.

Then my brothers told me that doctors don't bring babies. They told me women have babies like Ol' Lulu, my cat, has kittens. They said the kittens and babies were in their belly. When Lulu would have kittens, my brothers wouldn't let me watch, but I heard her meowing and crying in the closet. Soon there were baby kittens.

Later in the afternoon, the doctor came out of the house and said we had a new baby brother. Now I had ten brothers, no sisters. I ran into the house and got scared when I saw Mom was still in bed. The baby, Walter, was sleeping beside her. She said she was just tired, but she stayed in bed for several days, which I had never seen her do before. Daddy said she was OK, only needed to rest. He and the boys did the cooking, washing, and cleaning for a few days.

After the boys told me how babies came, I wondered about when I was born. I asked Mom to tell me about the time I was born after she was OK and up and around.

She said we lived a long way from town, too far for the doctor to get there, especially if the weather might be bad in the wintertime. Her neighbor and best friend, Goldie, helped moms have their babies. Late one night, Mom and Daddy sent an older brother to get Goldie. It was a cold winter night, and I was born very early in the morning. Mom said she heard my cry, and Daddy told her, "We have a tiny baby girl!"

Mom said she held me and went to sleep for a while. When she woke up, the boys and Daddy were gathered around her bed, laughing and talking. She said she looked out the bedroom window. The sun was coming up, and a beautiful blanket of snow covered the ground. She said she was so happy because she had a baby girl, her eighth child, but her first girl.

Because I was the first girl in the family, Mom said the boys told all the students and the teacher in the one-room country school. Daddy told all the neighbors he saw at the country store. The news quickly spread that the baby was a girl.

When my five brothers came home from school that day, they told Mom the other students wanted to name the new baby girl. Mom didn't have a girl's name picked out. One of my older brothers wanted to name me "Bonnie" after a little girlfriend he "claimed" in a former school. Mom agreed.

With Mom's approval, the teacher had the students in the school nominate several middle names, which she wrote on the blackboard. The students voted and chose "Mae," which was also Mom's middle name.

BLESSED MEMORIES OF GRANDPA LACEY

My first memory of Grandpa Lacey came at a bad time. When I was three years old, he rode with our family in the wagon to the cemetery to Earl's burial, one of my twin brothers who died at ten days.

The night before, I was asleep when hammering outside awakened me. I went to the window and saw Daddy nailing a lid on a small wooden box by lantern light. I went back to bed.

The next morning, we rode down a sandy road by team and wagon. Grandpa Lacey, my other brothers, and I were sitting in the wagon bed with the wooden box close by us. Daddy sat up front driving the horses. Mom and Grandma Lacey stayed home with baby Murrel.

We drove off the main road and stopped where there were big pretty rocks and stones in rows on the ground. My brothers said it was a cemetery. Daddy carried the box to where there was a deep hole in the ground. Some people were there, crying. The man in strange clothes said the baby went to Heaven. I didn't know where Heaven was, but I hoped I didn't go there. With ropes, they lowered the box into the hole in the ground and covered it with dirt.

The next day I watched Daddy pour wet cement into a small wooden box he made. He wrote some words in the cement and put many colorful shells around the writing. He said he was going to take it to Lil' Earl. The memories of that time are forever with me. But I did have many other good memories of Grandpa.

Edward Lacey (Ed) was born in Casey, Illinois, in 1866. He moved to Missouri as a youth, where he met my grandmother-to-be, Georganna (Annie) Sportsman, born in 1870. A few years after they were married, they moved to St. Clair County, Missouri, where they reared nine children, four girls, and five boys.

Grandpa and Grandma lived several miles away from where we lived in Cedar County. We didn't see them often because we didn't have a car. It took two hours to travel to their house by team and wagon. To communicate, we sent penny postcards to plan "get-to-gathers" at their home. My aunts, uncles, and cousins all got together, usually each fall and spring. There were over twenty cousins of all ages, our parents and Grandpa and Grandma.

For the get-to-gathers, the women cooked a large Sunday dinner. Grandpa and Grandma were vegetarian. Some of the families brought chicken and dumplings and sometimes a ham. We feasted on home-grown foods then we all went for the desserts. There were cakes and pies, especially pumpkin pies in the fall. After dinner, the men sat out on the porch drinking coffee. The women visited while they did the dishes. Kids of all ages enjoyed visiting and playing games.

Sometimes someone had a camera. There were pictures of family groups and bunches of cousins. By late afternoon, the families loaded the kids back in wagons and headed home to do chores. As we rode home, we were tired, still excited, and talking about the fun we had. These are special memories of my early childhood years.

It was the height of the Depression. One of Daddy's

brothers left the farm and moved to Milwaukee, Wisconsin, where there were relatives, and he could find work. Soon after, Grandpa and Grandma moved there, too, where he got a night-watchman's job in a factory.

When I was five years old, Grandma came to visit her family in our area. I didn't remember much about her before then. I noticed she was several inches taller than most women and "stocky," but not overweight. She was much bigger than Mom.

The weather was cold, and I remember her pulling a chair beside the heating stove and lighting a corncob pipe as she sat there to keep warm. I had heard of women smoking corncob pipes but didn't know that Grandma did. Grandpa didn't smoke or drink, not even coffee.

As she sat there, quiet and unsmiling, she seemed gruff and grumpy. When she talked, I noticed she had false teeth. That's what they called dentures then. The teeth were white, but they were set in plates that were black. Daddy said they used to make them of black rubber for people that didn't have much money. For people with money, the plates were made of silver. He said she was lucky to have false teeth. Some people had their teeth pulled and went without teeth because they couldn't afford false teeth.

After a couple of days, she visited her other families in the area and then went back to Milwaukee. Her visit hadn't been pleasant for us kids and, maybe, not for her either. I told my older brother, Jesse, who had already left home, how I felt. He said Grandma was really a kind and gentle woman. He had known her since his early childhood, and he loved her very much. I wished I had known her that way.

The next year, in 1937, when I was six years old,

Grandma died. She and Grandpa were married for over fifty years. She was brought back to Missouri for the funeral and burial. Daddy was wiping tears from his eyes with his handkerchief at the services, and I tried to cry for Daddy.

Grandpa missed the farm and working alongside Daddy and the boys. So, the next summer, he came to our farm. I remember him smiling and laughing much of the time. He was about Daddy's size, medium height, weight, and in good physical condition. He was seventy-two years young and ran footraces with my adolescent brothers and often won. We loved having him visit and missed him when he went back to Milwaukee.

A year later, Grandpa retired and moved to Joplin, Missouri, to be close to his oldest daughter, who lived in the area. She was married to a Seventh Day Adventist minister. He met a widow in the congregation, and they were soon married. Both were in their seventies. They settled on a small acreage outside of Joplin to grow his natural foods and keep a milk goat. Goat's milk was allowed in their diet. Our new Grandma liked cooking and canning, and they soon had a storehouse of canned foods.

When we left the farm and moved to Joplin in 1941, Grandpa lived across town from us. We visited him and our new Grandma most Sundays when Daddy was not working overtime.

I liked going through town on our way; I heard church bells ringing, making beautiful music. I had never heard church bells before. I really liked hearing them and wished I could go to church. We never went to church in Joplin.

We got to Grandpa's house late morning. He was usually out in his garden hoeing or picking tomatoes and other vegetables for Sunday Dinner. I was surprised because I knew he went to church, but Daddy said he went to church on Saturday. At ten years old, I didn't understand why.

Our new Grandma was a great cook and always prepared a big dinner. Our large family ate all we wanted. They didn't serve meat, but the veggies, fruits, grains, and beans provided a well-balanced diet.

I have many cherished memories of our times at Grandpa's house. We lived in Joplin for less than a year, where we were close to him. In the fall of 1942, we moved to Winchester, Kansas, where Daddy was recruited by a supervisor to do essential work in the war effort area. I only saw Grandpa a few more times after we moved away from Joplin.

The winter after Bill and I got married, his paint crew moved to southern Missouri to be in warmer weather. One Sunday morning, being close to Joplin, we decided to visit Grandpa and Grandma. I had his rural route address, but it had been about eight years since I was there, and I couldn't give clear directions.

The neighborhood where he lived was called Bacon Ridge. As we got close, I didn't recognize any landmarks. I asked Bill a couple of times to stop and ask where Bacon Ridge was. As is typical with men, he wouldn't consider asking directions. Finally, he said, "Oh, they'd just say, 'Look behind the pig's tail.'" Then I saw some familiar landmarks, and we found Grandpa's house.

Of course, Grandma insisted we stay for Sunday dinner. We had a special visit, and Bill got to meet my Grandpa.

Grandpa and our new Grandma lived a long healthy life together for over fifteen years. When he turned eighty-nine years, he and his wife both had to go to a nursing home, and they both died some weeks later within a few days of each other. It was in February 1954.

At that time, I was going to have our fourth child in June. My family didn't let me know that Grandpa and his wife had passed on. I didn't find out until several weeks later. I was distraught. When Mom told me, she said they had intentionally not told me. The weather was bad at the time, and she was concerned that I would have tried to travel the many miles to the memorial service anyway, no matter the weather. She was probably right.

The times I spent with Grandpa Lacey are blessed memories. I'll see him again someday.

Georganna "Annie" and Edward "Ed" Lacey
Wedding - late 1880s

Ed and Annie - 50th Anniversary

MY BUDDY AND MY BEST FRIEND

The story goes, when I was two months old, my brother Francis brought a Tabby kitty, two months old and just weaned, into the house for me. Mom didn't usually allow animals in the house, but she made an exception for the baby kitty. They said they named her Lulu. I only remember her being called Ol' Lulu by others; I called her Lulu.

In my first memories of Lulu, I was about three years old. I carried her with me almost everywhere I went. She was my buddy and my best friend. When someone scolded me, or I felt I was not "treated right," I picked her up and held her close. Sitting down on the floor behind the cookstove, I whispered my feelings to her. Lulu would snuggle close and purr like she understood. I'm sure she did.

It seemed Lulu and I always knew where each other was. If I was outside playing or inside helping Mom, Lulu was close by me, rubbing her soft fur against my legs and purring softly.

One day I saw Lulu outside the back, kitchen door, sitting on a wood stump. Spot, our hound dog, was slowly walking back and forth in front of her. She sat up and looked straight ahead like she was in charge. Spot continued moving closer, and then he began to walk toward her.

When Spot got close enough, Lulu reached out with her front paw and slapped him on his nose. He ran away, yelping loudly. But he didn't seem to learn. At times, over the years, the scene was repeated, and Lulu always won.

When our family left the farm, Lulu and I were ten years old. She rode in the car with me on the day long trip to Joplin. With all I was going through, from changing schools and the sadness of the start of World War II, Lulu was "My Buddy and My Best friend."

My family moved again in Joplin and then to Winchester, Kansas, when Lulu and I were twelve years old. Daddy hired a truck to move the furniture. He had a pickup, and he, Mom, and my little sister rode in the front seat. The boys and I rode in the back of the pickup, sitting on the floor. It was fun. Lulu was in a small cage close beside us, restless and wanting out.

The trip took several hours. When lunchtime came, Mom was prepared with sandwiches and drinks. We stopped at a roadside park in the country to eat. As we finished eating, Lulu was getting more and more restless, scratching on her cage door. Unexpectedly, my little brother opened the cage door, and Lulu took off like a streak into the nearby woods.

We ran after her, calling her name, but she had disappeared. We searched for over an hour, and we were all crying. Realizing we couldn't find her, Daddy said we had to move on.

Not having Lulu to hug was a big loss for me. I still miss "My Buddy and My Best Friend."

Lulu

MOM AND DADDY MAKE A FAMILY

Some would say that Mom was born on December 26, 1896, in Cedar County, Missouri into scandal and disgrace. They would be wrong.

While Anna Mae's mother was not married at the time, Maggie Barnard soon married William "Billie" Stroer. As Mom grew up, her mother never, ever, told her he was not her father. She found out through rumors when she was an adolescent. She had always adored her "Poppy," but loved and respected him even more after knowing he willingly became her "Father."

As Mom was growing up, she realized the community and the local church they attended respected her mother and Poppy. Over time they added ten more children to their family.

Mom only went to school through the fourth grade, as was common then. Being the oldest child in a large family and being a girl, she had a short childhood, often doing a grownup's work at an early age. At fourteen years of age, she met and married a man who was several years older. Because of a birth abnormality, it limited him in the work he could do. He and Mom lived with his grandmother for several years through mutual agreement beneficial to all.

They attended church regularly, which pleased Mom as she had grown up in the church. She said she soon "decided to follow Jesus" and became a member of the church. She loved the singing and memorized the hymns, which were sermons in themselves, and she often sang in the kitchen while she worked when I was a child.

Her husband's grandmother taught Mom homemaking skills while living with them as she "grew up," especially cooking. Mom said the grandmother was an excellent cook and showed her how to use special seasonings and spices in main dishes, desserts, and bread. They never wrote down the recipes, just kept them in their heads. Mom became recognized throughout her lifetime by extended family and neighbors for her fine cooking.

Mom had her first baby, a boy when she was seventeen years old. Over the next ten years, she and her husband added four more sons to their family, making five sons. Then the grandmother died, leaving Mom, her husband, and sons without a place to live, making for difficult times for her family. There are many stories about the circumstances, but eventually, Mom and her husband divorced. To add to the difficulty, Mom said she was "kicked out of the church" because of the divorce. She could not even attend when she needed them the most.

Having no place to go, Mom and the boys moved back to Cedar County to live with her parents. Her mother's two youngest children were about the same age as Mom's two youngest sons.

Daddy had a hard life but made the best of it. He taught us to be thankful for what you have.

Herbert Lewis Lacey was born in Texas County, Missouri, on a farm on December 18, 1893, into a large family. In his childhood, the family moved to Reno County, Kansas, then to Cedar County, Missouri. I know little about his early childhood, except that they lived in a remote area with only eighth-grade schools. There were no high schools close enough to attend because there were not enough students.

At that time, most students didn't go to high school. They believed a fourth-grade education was all that was necessary. By that grade, most students could read, write, and do simple arithmetic. And by twelve years of age, they were often needed to help with housework or help on the farm where most of them lived.

The boys who stayed in school longer didn't start the school year until the harvest was over and only attended until planting time in early spring, about four full months. Because of not completing an entire school year, some attended grade school until they were in their teens or even early twenties.

Daddy, however, finished and graduated from grade school, even though he said he had to do the short school year. He may have been in his late teens when he finished. He said that because he made good grades and was as big as the older boys, the school district official persuaded him to take "Postgraduate" classes and get a teaching certificate to teach in the country schools. They preferred men teachers. It was sometimes difficult to recruit women teachers when many of the students were bigger than the women.

He taught school for a few years. His family lived on the adjoining farm of another large family. Eventually, he and two of his brothers married three sisters from that family.

In less than a year, Daddy's wife died in childbirth, and the baby was stillborn. In that remote area, often self-appointed midwives delivered babies because there were no doctors or nurses available. The outcome for his wife, and many other women, was tragically common.

Then, he decided to follow the harvest, which took him "out west" to Kansas, Oklahoma, and Texas. The workers found out that he had taught school. So, at night, he taught some illiterate people to read, write, and do simple math. Also, somewhere he had learned how to cut hair and provided this extra service for the men who wanted to look neat when the harvest crews were close enough to go to town. He made a little extra money doing the services, a great advantage for him.

When he and the crew were in town, he watched a traveling theatre put on a stage show. The stage performance intrigued him. When he found that they paid better than harvesting paid, he joined the group. They traveled through several states west of Missouri. He was glad to get the experience, and many considered him, "Well Traveled." After a couple of years, he went back to Cedar County, where his family lived.

Not long after returning to Cedar County, he "courted" a young woman he had known before, and they were soon married. Tragedy struck again. About a year later, his second wife and a baby died in childbirth.

Daddy's second wife was a sister to Anna Mae Stroer, who became his third wife and would later become my mother. Anna had recently divorced, which most churches considered an "unpardonable sin." She had five sons and was living with her parents in the area. Before long, she, Herbert, and the boys moved to Jasper County, Missouri, near Joplin, where they married. Daddy worked for a farmer there.

About a year later, their first son together, James, was born. In 1927, there was heavy recruiting for workers in the mines in Pitcher, Oklahoma. Because the pay was good, they moved there, by team and wagon, a several hour drive.

After he had worked for many months in the mines, there was a cave-in while he was deep inside. They rescued him but carried him out for dead on a stretcher. He was unconscious, but later they told him he roused enough to ask, "Did anyone get hurt in this accident?" Thinking he was dead, the men carrying him were so startled and frightened they dropped the stretcher with Daddy on it and briefly ran away. Soon they returned and took him to the hospital. He fully recovered but had large scars over his back after he healed.

In 1929, my parents had another son, Robert. The Stock Market crashed soon after that, and Daddy had recovered from the accident. When the depression set in, they moved back to Cedar County, so Daddy and the boys could raise our food to keep from going hungry. He worked for other farmers, did sharecropping and rented a farm for the crop shares.

I was born on the farm in 1931, the eighth child and the first girl. In the following years, they had four more sons: Fredrick, Murrel, Earl, and Walter and a second daughter, Carol Marie. Earl, one of the twins died after only ten days.

Anna Mae Stroer (12) with siblings

Anna Mae Stroe, age 16

Herbert "Herb" Lacey, age 17

Herb Lacey in 20s

THE MULBERRY TREE

The boys are climbing the mulberry tree, picking the big, juicy berries and eating 'em. Now they're throwing some down so I can pick 'em up and eat 'em. They are so juicy and sweet as sugar! I want to climb the tree, too.

My big brothers tell me, "No, 'cause you might fall! Mom don't want you to show yer bloomers."

Like my brother about my size, I can hold on like him, and I'd like to wear overhalls like the boys do. I think I will climb the mulberry tree sometime.

I wake up smelling the good breakfast Mom was fixing; hot biscuits and gravy. We all eat a big breakfast because Daddy and the boys are going out in the fields today to hoe the corn and 'taters. Then they leave, and Mom washes the dishes. When I get bigger, I will help her. Mom says I just had a birthday, and now I am three years old. But I'm too little to help. I want to get bigger soon.

I run outside and don't see Daddy and the boys anywhere. I will climb the mulberry tree today. Climbing is really hard. It's hard to hold on around the tree because it's so big. My arms and legs are so short, and my dress tail git's in the way. Now it's better because I can use the limbs to git up into the middle of the tree where the berries are. The berries are sweet, and the juice is running down my arms. It's cool up here because it's still morning and the sun is not hot yet.

Mom is calling me!

"Bonnie Mae, wher' are you?"

Why is she yelling at me? She only says "Bonnie Mae" when she's mad at me! Why is she so mad at me? She sounds so scared! I holler back, "I'm up in the mulberry tree!"

She's hollering back, "What?"

Why is she yelling so loud? Here she comes, hurrying! She's trying to run fast!

She's still yelling! "What are you doin' up in the tree? Be careful, or you'll fall! Git down! Be careful! Don't catch yer dress tail or you might fall! Little girls are not supposed to climb trees! You're showin' yer bloomers! Little girls like you are not supposed to show their bloomers!"

I asked, "Why can't I wear overhalls?"

She says, "Girls are not supposed to wear boy's clothes. It's not ladylike."

I wonder what ladylike means, but I don't ask. I climbed down. Why is she so mad and sounds scared too?

Mom is underneath the tree now. She says, "Yer not supposed to go where I can't see you! Why are you climbin' trees?"

I tell her, "I saw the boys climbin' trees yesterday, and they wouldn't let me climb 'cause I would show my bloomers. They're out workin' where they can't see my bloomers. So now I can climb and eat mulberries."

As I get to the ground, Mom takes me by the hand and leads me to the well's big flat rock. It's where she has me sit when she's mad at me. That's better than getting' a spankin' like the boys do sometimes.

She tells me, "Sit down here on the rock 'til I tell you git up! Don't move! I want to see you from the kitchen window while I'm cookin' dinner! I want you to think about what you did."

I still don't know why she is so mad at me and so scared! Why can't girls do what boys do? I don't want to be a boy. I just want to do what boys do, like climbing trees, riding horses, and getting haircuts.

Mom had me sit on the rock once before. It was when Daddy cut the boys' hair but wouldn't cut mine. It got so tangled and hurt when Mom combed it. So, when Daddy cut the boys' hair, I watched where he put the scissors. When they left, and I was alone, I cut my hair. I heard Mom calling my name, and I crawled under the bed. When she saw my hair on the floor, she yelled, "Bonnie Mae!" As I crawled from under the bed, she started crying. She set me on the stool and trimmed my hair. She looked sad and took me by the hand, took me to the big flat rock, and made me sit for a long time.

Now I've been sitting here for a long time for climbing the mulberry tree. Now Daddy and boys are coming in from the fields for dinner. Mom says I can git up and come into the kitchen to eat with them. I see Daddy and the boys are sweaty and dirty. I don't want to get so sweaty, but I still want to wear overhalls, ride horses and climb trees. But I'm glad I don't have to hoe corn and 'taters.

Bonnie

MY EARLY MEMORIES

In June 1934, when I was three years old, I remember climbing the Mulberry tree. I recall cutting my hair a few weeks before. I have many memories of living on the farm.

On July 17th of the same year, the doctor came to our house on the farm. Daddy was sick. My brothers said the doctor would make Daddy's blood poisoning better. After a while, the doctor came out of the front door smiling, picked me up, and told me I had two new baby brothers. I went into the bedroom to see the new babies. Mom was holding a baby on each arm and smiling. Neighbor women were standing nearby, fanning Mom and the babies, Murrel and Earl.

The doctor came back ten days later. When he left the house, he was not smiling. My brothers told me that Lil' Earl had died. By then, Daddy was feeling better. But our hearts ached for the loss.

That year the Midwest had the worst drought ever recorded in our country. Dust from the Dust Bowl in Kansas blew across Kansas into Washington, DC. Farmers' crops planted in the spring didn't grow because it hadn't rained for months. People and animals were starving and dying from a lack of available food.

One day in late summer, rain clouds started forming in the sky, and the winds started blowing. Mom was outside watching with us. We were barefoot, running about, and playing. The animals and chickens were moving around restlessly. They seemed to sense the weather was changing.

The clouds continued to form. Mom said it really looked like it was going to rain. I didn't remember ever seeing rain. The chickens and animals continued moving around restlessly. Strong winds started blowing and raindrops began to fall softly. Soon it was falling fast and hard. We stayed out in the rain with our hair and clothes dripping wet. We kicked and splashed in the puddles with the rain falling on our faces.

The rains in 1934 that covered most of the Midwest were over by late summer. It was too late to plant most crops that would have time to grow before winter. Daddy and the boys plowed the fields and planted many acres of turnips, which grew fast. They pulled up wagon loads of turnips and stored them for our family and the many animals for the winter. He fed turnips to the horses, cows, and pigs. The cow's milk and the sausage tasted like turnips. We also shared turnips with our neighbors.

It started getting too cold to play outside barefoot. Mom said it was wintertime, and it would be cold for a long time. We put on our shoes, long socks, and long underwear. The fires in the kitchen and front room stove kept us warm in the day time, even though the cold winds blew through the cracks and around the windows and doors. Daddy stoked the fires with extra wood at night and closed the dampers, but the fires still burned down. The boys snuggled together under heavy quilts. Daddy and Mom slept with my two-year-old brother, the baby, and me to keep us from getting cold and safe from rodents.

It was common in rural communities for rodents to come into houses in the wintertime. Rats could and would gnaw holes through the floors. If babies were not well protected at night, rats would get into their beds and chew on their noses, fingers, and toes, grossly disfiguring them. Because Mom and Daddy slept with my two baby brothers and me, we were never bothered.

Winter was about over, and it started to get warm. We were excited and busy packing boxes and loading furniture on the wagons to take to our new house, which Daddy and my brothers were building a few miles away. It took many trips to move furniture, farm equipment, and animals. There were pigs, chickens, cows, and horses. The horses pulled the wagons and the farm equipment, and the boys rode them to herd the cows. The wagons hauled the pigs and chickens.

One wagon was loaded, with enough room for my little brothers and me to ride in the wagon bed. Mom rode up front holding the baby. An older brother drove us to our new home. Down the dirt road and across the little shallow creek we went. Then I saw the big new log barn Daddy and my brothers built. As we drove past it, the new house came into sight.

That evening the animals were fed, and the cows milked. The rest of us unloaded the furniture, the kitchen stove, and dining table. Tired and hungry, we feasted on cornbread Mom made ahead of time and fresh cows' milk. The boys set up our parents' bed for them, and the rest of us slept on pallets on the new wooden floors.

The dining room was between the kitchen and the front

room. There was a floor, a roof, and a framework on the sides, but that was all. Squirrels came down from the trees and played on the framework. Daddy and the boys were busy plowing and planting spring crops. Before winter, they took the time to enclose the dining room.

They cultivated the land for the first time. They cut down trees, plowed around the stumps, and planted the garden and fields. I didn't recall having so many kinds of food before. There were root crops, leaf crops, tomatoes, corn, beans, and peas.

The Morel Mushrooms grew wild in the swampy ground below the house in the spring. Wild blackberries ripened in mid-summer. There were persimmons and wild grapes. Rare and most unusual, though, were the pawpaw trees and their fruit. They looked somewhat like a large, pale green egg. When they were ripe and soft, we picked them and ate them out of hand. They were so unusual and delicious.

Our farm became a favorite gathering place for our neighbors. One day Daddy came home in the wagon, from the country store, with our groceries and feed for the animals. I saw him lifting a big, clear block out of the wagon. He said we were going to have a neighborhood ice cream party. He broke off little chunks of ice, and I picked up a small chip and started sucking on it. I decided to save a piece for the next day. I hid a small chunk of ice in a hole in the foundation of the house.

Neighbors arrived in their wagons, but some were walking because they had no horses or cars. Mom mixed the ice cream from our fresh cow's milk and Daddy poured it into the freezer buckets. The boys hand-cranked the freezers until the ice cream was frozen. There was enough for everyone to have all they wanted. The neighbors visited, and the kids ran and played games. It was the first of many pleasant summer evenings with neighbors.

After a night's sleep, I woke up thinking about the ice I hid the night before, but it was gone when I checked. I was upset and told Daddy someone took my ice. He smiled and said, "No, it melted like the snow in winter." I didn't know what he meant until winter came, and the snow and ice melted, just like he said it would. I was four years old.

Daddy's greatest concern was for our safety. When he was a young man, a friend his age drowned, so he wanted us to know how to swim. We had swimming holes in the creek on our farm, a favorite place for my brothers. They enjoyed it from early spring until frost in the fall. Sometimes they swam after our noon meal, while Daddy lingered at the table drinking coffee.

After a long day in the fields, the boys jumped into the swimming hole to "wash off" before coming to the barn to do the chores. They could do that because they went "skinny-dippin," with no women or girls around to see them. I did learn to swim, but because the boys wanted to skinny-dip, they did not welcome me. They didn't have bathing suits, so they had to wear overalls when I went with them.

One unpleasant memory is etched forever in my mind. As a child, I heard people talking about getting drunk. I didn't know what they were talking about until one winter night, when   I was five years old, and my family had gone to bed.

We woke up to crying and loud banging on our kitchen door. Mom and Daddy hurried to the door. I followed close behind. Daddy's sister and her daughter my age were at the door in their nightclothes, barefoot with no coats or caps; the snow was several inches deep. We brought them in by the fire and gave them some of my and Mom's warm clothes.

My aunt told us her husband got drunk, mad at them, and ran them out of the house. They had to run in the snow from their house to ours, about half a mile away. My uncle was usually polite and pleasant. I had never seen anyone drunk and hoped I never did again. My aunt and cousin stayed with us that night. My uncle came the next morning and took them home with him. I will always remember how my uncle treated my aunt and cousin that night.

The square dances every year in the fall were fun times in our community. Neighbors gathered at one family's house for a dance. They usually moved some furniture out into the yard to make room for dancing, then moved it back in after the dance.

Some friends played instruments: guitars, fiddles, banjos, harmonicas, and usually a washboard for rhythm. At times there was only one instrument. Several men knew how to call the square dances. Men, women, and children joined in, usually forming two or three square dance groups. After square dancing for a while, the musicians, or musician, would start a waltz, two-step, a jig dance, or clog dance. Everyone joined in, especially Mom and Daddy.

In late summer, the neighbors enjoyed getting together at our house for a "Watermelon Feast" outside. Daddy grew wagon loads of watermelons, which he hauled to town and sold. There were always enough melons to have neighbors over for a feast. They sliced the long melons lengthwise, and we ate them with our hands, juice dripping off our elbows. Neighbors visited among themselves, and the kids played games. By late evening, the families started home, some of them by team and wagon, but some walked a mile or more because they had no horses or cars.

One thing I loved doing was helping Mom. I wanted to help her like my brothers did. Starting at about the age of five, I would set the table then go to the kitchen where Mom was cooking breakfast, often biscuits and gravy. I wanted to stir the gravy for her, but I was too short to safely reach the spoon handle. When I asked to help her, she said, "No, you're too little."

One day Daddy came into the kitchen with a small wooden box, just the right size for me to stand on beside the stove to help stir the gravy, so Mom had told him what I wanted to do. She began by getting the gravy started and stirred it until it got thick enough so it wouldn't lump. I would stand on the box and stir the gravy while she did other things she needed to do. I felt so important.

I loved to wander around in the woods by myself. One morning when I was six years old, I was outside below the house gathering greens. I picked a bucket full of them and started picking pretty wildflowers for Mom. Having been out most of the morning, I realized I needed to go to the outhouse, but I was a long way from it.

I had seen my brothers go behind a tree when they didn't know I was looking. They didn't think I knew what they were doing. I found a big tree, pulled down my bloomers, and squatted behind the tree when no one was looking, or so I thought. I soon realized I had to do a complete job. After finishing, I cleaned myself with fresh leaves, stood up, and pulled up my bloomers.

Our old hound dog was standing close by. I looked at him and said, "Sic 'um Spot, sic 'um!" And he did! Suddenly an older brother jumped out from behind a tree nearby and started laughing at me. My brother told that story about Ol' Spot and me at family gatherings for as long as he lived.

Since we didn't have a bathroom, they favored Mom and me when it came to our going to the outhouse, especially at night and in the winter. We used a bucket that we kept under the bed, and the boys emptied in the morning. One day Daddy brought home a beautiful, hand-painted porcelain commode that he bought at an auction. He said they were used by "proper women" that lived in fancy houses, so they didn't have to go to the outhouse. He placed it in the corner where I slept on a cot in my parents' bedroom. At night, when the weather got cold, Mom and I made good use of the commode.

One cold winter evening, the family had gathered around the stove in the front room. In our bedroom close by, I decided I needed to use the commode. The flared rim fit just right for me to sit on it. Sitting there, I took hold of the rim and pulled myself a little way into the opening. As the air in the commode went past me, it made a sound like I was doing my job. I pushed on the rim, and it made a sucking sound, almost like the first one. The boys got quiet, and then they started laughing; I did it again and again while they laughed. I occasionally repeated the performance to provide a little laughter on an otherwise long, cold, and quiet winter night.

As I watched Mom, it seemed like she could do everything. Besides cooking most of the time, she had a treadle sewing machine where she spent many evenings sewing. I would stand at her elbow and watch her sew our dresses and bloomers. Daddy bought the animals' feed in printed sacks in the patterns Mom wanted until she had enough matching sacks to make our clothes. She had patterns she cut from newspapers.

When I was eight years old, I started watching how she peddled the sewing machine and moved the material under the needle to sew the cloth together. I begged her to let me sew my bloomers. Soon she cut the fabric for a pair of bloomers and let me try to sew them. Sewing was hard for me at first. My peddling was uneven; the machine would jerk, then stall and cause the thread to break. I would get upset, then thread the needle and try again, not willing to give up. Eventually, I was sewing the pieces together and finishing a pair of bloomers. Soon I was sewing other seams for Mom.

The sewing soon came in handy for me. I always wanted to go swimming, but the boys liked to skinny-dip, so that I couldn't go with them. Mom said if I wanted to go swimming with the boys, I could make swimsuits out of white feed sacks with my bloomer pattern. She showed me how to adjust the pattern to make different sizes. My brothers were not happy about it.

We had two swimming holes: The Big Hole and the Little hole. After I made their swimsuits, the boys would stay with me at the Little Hole, which was not very deep. Sometimes they would take me with them to the Big Hole that was deep, and the water was rough and cold.

After I learned to swim in the Little Hole, they talked me into staying there while they went out of my sight to the Big Hole to skinny-dip. They made me promise not to tell Mom or Daddy what they did. I didn't care because the water was not so deep and was warmer in the Little Hole. If Mom or Daddy had ever found out about it, the boys would have been in a heap of trouble.

One of the most significant happenings in Cedar County was the El Dorado Springs Picnic, which was held every year for three days around the middle of July. Our family went together to town in the morning by team and wagon for the first time to the picnic. When we got there, Daddy tied the horses up, and the boys and I ran the short distance to the picnic carnival and festivities in the center of the small town.

Crowds of people were walking around eating and talking. There were game booths, a Ferris wheel, a merry-go-round, and other rides. Food booths and ice cream stands lined the streets. Daddy gave each of the boys and me two dimes, from a roll of dimes he had, to spend as we chose.

I headed for the merry-go-round with all the pretty toy horses. They were not busy that morning, so the man let me and others ride longer than usual. I was so thrilled. I paid my dime and rode a long time, one dime gone. Then I went to the ice cream stand, where I bought a large cone with three ice cream flavors: my first ice cream cone and my last dime.

But there were lots of other things to see and do. The park across the street had sidewalks and grass where we could run and play while music played in the pavilion in the center of the park. Springs of water ran out of a hillside where we could take a tin cup and get a cold drink. There were benches throughout the sloping hillsides where the people sat in the shade to watch the entertainment. The local high school band, in uniform, played—my first time to hear or see horns and drums. There were groups singing cowboy songs and folk songs.

Lunchtime came, but the food there cost too much for our large family. Mom packed a large basket with sandwiches she made with boiled, seasoned, and ground chicken on sourdough bread. She also included her wonderful cinnamon rolls.

We sat on a quilt on the ground in the shady park and feasted and listened to the music. When late afternoon came, we loaded back into the wagon and headed home to do the evening chores. We went to the picnic other times after that, but I shall always remember that wonderful first time at the picnic.

My rowdy brothers knew how to have fun. The summer I was eight years old, just before the Fourth of July, an older brother saw that I had coins. I had saved them from people who gave me pennies and nickels just because I was the only girl in the family. He said the coins would buy a lot of firecrackers. Even though I didn't know what firecrackers were, I gave him the handful of coins, and he bought hundreds of inch-long firecrackers called Lady Fingers.

We had fun shooting firecrackers all day long on the Fourth of July. It was fun for me, getting to do what boys do. Before the day was over, Mom was getting upset with the noise, especially when my brothers would sneak up under the kitchen window where she was working, light a firecracker, and make her jump. She would yell at them to stop, and they did for a while, then they would do it again. That was the only time I ever knew that the boys didn't mind Mom. But I believe that if she had really wanted to stop them, she would have. She humored them in their fun.

I had wanted to learn to ride a bicycle ever since I saw a girl riding a bike on my first day of school. I didn't know how she could keep it from falling over. One day an older brother brought home a boy's old rusty bicycle without tires. He planned to paint the bike and save some money to buy new tires. He stored it in the hayloft of the barn.

Daddy and the boys were working out in the fields. I decided to see if I could ride the bike. I went to the barn, tied a rope to the bike's crossbar, and lowered it to the ground. I pushed it to the big tree by the path to the house and climbed onto it. My feet didn't touch the peddles when I sat on the seat, so I wrapped burlap feed sacks around the crossbar, sat on it and reached the peddles.

I sat on the padded crossbar and pushed off with my foot from the tree down the house's gentle slope. Going fast so I would stay upright, I soon realized I didn't know how to steer it. I panicked and ran into the side of the house. Mom came to the door, saw I wasn't hurt, and went back inside.

Though shaken, I pushed the bike back up to the tree. Climbing on, I did the same thing, hitting the house. After several tries, I figured out how to turn the handlebars, miss the house, and peddle a short distance down the house's sandy road.

One day I was able to keep peddling past an open gate and go all the way to our neighbor's house before I fell over. I couldn't get back on the bike without the tree, so I pushed it back home, about a quarter of a mile away. By then, I had completely ruined the wheels, but my brother didn't seem to care. After knowing I could ride the bike, the new wore off, and I went on to other challenges. But I had learned to ride it, just like the girl at school, well, almost.

June 10, 1940 was one of the most important and memorable days of my life. At nine years old, I had ten living brothers and no sisters, until that day. Carol Marie changed our lives, especially mine.

In late June of 1941, I was having pains in my lower right side. Two of my brothers had appendicitis at different times. My pain wasn't as severe as my brothers' pain was, but Mom and Daddy decided to have an older brother drive Daddy and me in his car, to Kansas City to the Children's Mercy

Hospital. Daddy's sister lived close to the hospital. She could visit me and take me to stay with her if they dismissed me before Daddy could come to take me home.

When we went inside the hospital, I became really scared. After the doctors examined me and Daddy admitted me, he and my brother had to leave to go back to the farm. I was still afraid, but the doctors and nurses treated me nicely. I don't know what the medicine was they gave me, but the pain went away after a few days.

I heard the doctors and nurses talking about the fireworks display on the Fourth of July. One day I heard the staff saying it was the Fourth of July, and the fireworks display would be that evening. The staff and some family members helped us go outside to chairs set up on the lawn.

When it was nearly dark, a band started playing the National Anthem. Everyone who could stand stood, and we sang the Star-Spangled Banner and saluted the flag. Suddenly the fireworks display started. It seemed like the beautiful, bright, and colorful lights covered the whole sky and flashed for a long time in the night sky. That evening is another beautiful memory.

A few days later, I was dismissed from the hospital and went to stay with my aunt. It was my introduction to "city life." She lived in an apartment, which was a lot nicer than our house, but I didn't like the city because there were no trees or grass, only concrete streets and sidewalks. And my aunt's cooking wasn't as good as Mom's. Daddy and my brother came to take me home, and I was glad to be back on the farm where there was grass and trees and flowers. And fresh food that didn't come in boxes and cans.

I have dozens of cousins, no exaggeration. Most of

them lived in the city. Each summer, four or five of them spent their summers on the farm with us, both boys and girls. They ranged in age from eight years to sixteen years.

Daddy and Mom expected them to do their fair share of the work, and they did. The older boys worked with Daddy and the boys in the fields and garden and learned to take care of animals. The cousins liked riding horses and swimming. The older girls helped Mom in the kitchen, learning cooking, bread making, and canning. And they had time to play just like my brothers and I did. The younger kids spent their time playing with my little brothers and me. I liked having girl playmates.

I was so scared when I heard people talking about a world war.

Daddy started working from the farm, doing carpenter work, helping build military training bases, ammunition plants, even prisoner of war camps in Missouri. He was gone for weeks at a time until he got a car. Then he came home most weekends when he didn't have to work overtime.

My brothers at home were old enough to care for the animals, some crops, and gardening. After a few months, Daddy and Mom decided to have an auction of the animals and the farm equipment. Managing the farm was too much for the boys without Daddy there.

I was both excited and anxious about moving. The family would be close to where Daddy was working. We were all looking forward to that. But I was worried about leaving my friends and the only school and teacher I had ever known. And anxious about going to the "Big City" and leaving the farm "where I grew up." I was ten years old.

When we left the farm, a world and a life opened for me that I didn't know existed, sometimes good and sometimes not so good. The years on the farm, however, with Mom's and Daddy's teaching by example, prepared me well to deal with life's situations and problems and to enjoy and appreciate life and my blessings.

WHOLE BROTHERS IN EVERY WAY

My five older brothers had a tremendous impact on my early years and my life. They seemed to like having a little sister to spoil, and they never stopped.

These brothers had a different father than I had, not that it ever mattered. They helped me feel safe, secure, and happy… not that they may have favored me and spoiled me since I was their first and only sister.

Jesse once told me this story: When he was young, his father's sister asked him why he wanted to live with my family instead of his father. Jesse said, "I told her, I have horses to ride and plenty of food to eat and besides… I have a baby sister."

The two older boys stayed with their father after he and Mom were divorced, and the three younger boys went with Mom. After Mom and Daddy married, the two older boys came to live with us on the farm. They were nine and twelve years old. The boys were all taken in and fully accepted by Daddy's family, and they liked living on the farm.

DON: He once told me he enjoyed working with Daddy, learning to farm, gardening, carpentry, care of animals, and many other essential life skills. When I first remember Don, he worked like a man alongside Daddy, sawing, and cutting trees to build our new home.

Not long after our family moved to our new house,

Don brought his girlfriend, Clara, to visit us for the day. We had known her since childhood, but I didn't know she would be Don's girlfriend. She was so nice to me, giving me one of her childhood dolls. Clara was beautiful. She had long dark hair and beautiful clothes she made herself. She would soon become my brother's wife. I decided she would be "My First Sister."

They were married and lived in a one-room cottage that Don built in the meadow on our farm. They went to California, as many others did, to find work during the Depression. They started out with Clara's older brother in a Model T Ford pickup. The top speed was about 25 miles per hour, so it took a while to get there.

When the economy started getting better in the Midwest, they moved back to Missouri, where Don worked for a farmer. Then they moved to Columbus, Kansas, where his father and family lived. He started his own business as a carpenter, building houses, and was very successful. Daddy had taught him carpentry and was proud of Don's accomplishments.

After a few years, Don and Clara moved to Wichita, Kansas, to work in the aircraft industry as the country was gearing up for WW II. He sometimes spoke of regretting not going into the military as his brothers did. His work, however, was just as essential for the war effort as the military was.

Don and Clara reared five children, two girls, and three boys, a beautiful family. With Clara's help, he became the head of our extended family. When the war was over, most of our extended family moved to Wichita, where wages were good. Many of them moved in with Don and Clara and their family until they could settle into their own home. Don lived life to the fullest, and his family, siblings, and friends miss him.

JESSE: My second brother was second only in birth order. I remember him helping Daddy on the farm, learning all the skills his older brother learned. He often played games with me and showed me a lot of attention.

When he was eighteen years old, he joined the newly founded Civilian Conservation Corps, known as CC Camp, a program developed during the Depression for young men between the ages of eighteen and twenty years. They sent them away to for a year to work for the National Forest and Park Service in many parts of the country to learn working skills and earn money, thirty-three dollars a month. Fifteen dollars a month of that was sent home to parents, a lot of money. It was a great help in covering expenses on the farm.

Soon after coming home from CC Camp, Jesse joined the army and became a Medic. When he came home on leave, he brought Mom and me little gifts. The first I recall was a gold-framed copy of John 3:16 for Mom that she hung on the wall.

But the gift I remember best was the anatomy book he brought me from where he worked as a Medic. I was six years old and couldn't read big books, but I looked at the pictures and asked him to tell me about them. I was so excited to see what we look like inside. When I asked what girls do where he works, he said, "They are nurses, and they help people feel better." I decided right then I wanted to be a nurse when I grew up.

While in the Army, Jesse met and married a beautiful

young woman, Bonnie, and had a baby boy. Soon WWII started, and he was sent overseas and served in heavy combat zones in Europe. He and his fellow medics went into the battlefields to rescue the wounded and carry them back to safety for treatment. He came through it all without injury.

When Jesse came home from the war, he left the Army, and he and Bonnie had another son. He started into construction work on roads and soon became foreman. One day he and his crew were working under a railroad overpass when an unscheduled train came through, and the scaffolding collapsed on him, pinning him under it. When they rescued him, he was not breathing. They didn't think he was alive but started CPR by doing back-thrusts. His back was broken, and the back-thrusts severed his spinal cord. Nevertheless, they saved his life. Jesse went through extended therapy to learn to walk again with braces but eventually decided to remain in the wheelchair.

Jesse was paraplegic at age thirty-five. He had an amazing attitude and was an inspiration to all who knew him, much of it made possible by his wonderful wife, who stood by him. With adaptive tools, he did gardening and once painted his house. He bought a motorboat to go fishing and pull water skiers, of which I was one. Jesse had a lot of standby help, and he and all involved had many good times. He lived life to the fullest and didn't let much stop him.

LONNIE: When he was about twelve years old, he started complaining about a "bellyache." He could hardly walk or stand up straight. Mom and Daddy said he must have appendicitis. We didn't have a car. Daddy asked our neighbor farmer, who had a pickup truck, to take

Lonnie and Daddy to the closest hospital in Fort Scott, Kansas, about forty miles away. They loaded him in the pickup's bed, on quilts for a mattress, and went to the hospital.

The hospital did an emergency appendectomy, and they told Daddy Lonnie's appendix had burst, spreading infection throughout his body. Daddy had to leave Lonnie there so he and his neighbor could come back home. I heard Daddy tell Mom that the doctors didn't know whether Lonnie would live.

We didn't have a phone and had to rely on the hospital to call our neighbor to keep us informed. Lonnie had to stay in the hospital for about two weeks until he was well enough to come home. Mom went with our neighbor to bring Lonnie home.

Daddy realized, when Lonnie was a teenager, that he would faint at the sight of blood. One day Daddy was cleaning a bloody wound on a horse and had Lonnie holding the reins to keep the horse from moving. The horse started moving. Daddy looked up and saw Lonnie had fainted and fell when he saw blood.

When Lonnie turned eighteen, he went to CC Camp for a year, and he and my family received the same benefits we received from his older brother: Work experience and thirty-three dollars pay each month, with fifteen dollars sent home to the family.

After Lonnie came home from CC Camp, he courted and married Alean, his lovely childhood sweetheart. When WWII started, they drafted him into the army. As he and others were having their physicals, he fainted at the sight of blood as the recruits were getting their shots. They decided that he could not go into combat, so they put him into Quartermasters after basic training. Quartermasters consisted of providing services and supplies to the troops.

As he was finishing basic training, Lonnie's Sargent allowed him to go home on special leave because Alean was about to have their baby. Soon after he arrived home, the baby boy was born. After a few days, Lonnie had to go overseas. He did not see his wife and son again for over four years until the war was over.

Lonnie was the only brother injured, and that was after the war was over. He tripped a booby-trap that put shrapnel in his chest. After the wound healed, he was discharged and returned home and settled into life on the farm with his wife. They added another son to their family. Eventually, they moved to Wichita, where he built their house with his brothers' help, and he went to work for the railroad.

Lonnie is no longer with us, but I have remained in close contact with his sons.

FRANCIS: He did farm work with his brothers and often helped Mom in the kitchen. He was usually close by me, assuring I was safe. The day I started to our one-room country school, my other brothers ran on ahead of me. Francis waited for me, and we started walking, holding hands. I was five years old, small for my age, and couldn't take very long steps.

He picked me up under my arms and put me on his back. We were both barefoot. He told me to put my feet in his overalls' hip-pockets and hold on around his neck. He ran, carrying me on his back the mile or so to the schoolhouse. For several weeks he continued to carry me to school until I was comfortable going by myself.

The day he went away to CC Camp, my younger brothers and I lined up crying, to hug and kiss him goodbye. We had not done that for the other brothers. We knew how much we would miss him.

When he came back from CC Camp, he went to work for a local farmer who had three pretty daughters. He courted Violet, who was nearest his age. They soon fell in love and were married. They moved to Joplin, Missouri, where he worked with Daddy, who was working, building a military base.

When they declared WWII, Francis and Violet moved back to Cedar County to the farm where a daughter and a son were born. Eventually, Francis was drafted into the Army. They sent him overseas with thousands of other recruits to replace our troops' losses in the Battle of the Bulge. He was in heavy combat for many months until they declared the war over. Thankfully, he didn't suffer any injuries.

When he returned home, he and his wife and family settled back on the farm in Missouri. After a year or so, he moved his family to Wichita, as others of our extended family had done, because work prospects and wages were good. He went to work in a meatpacking plant. They bought an acreage and built a new home. He and his wife reared a family of one boy and six girls. Francis always had large gardens, which kept the whole family busy... not always to the kids' liking.

When Bill and I moved our family to Wichita, Francis' family and my family spent many fun times together. Along with our other family members, we frequently gathered at our house for family dinners. But square dances in our big old Victorian house was the most fun. On many Saturday nights, we would all dance until two o'clock in the morning with Francis calling the square dances. Although he is no longer with us, his children have stayed in touch and close.

ALVIN: The youngest of the five older brothers, Alvin, also helped Mom in the kitchen. He let me work along beside him, even though I was just six years old. He made me feel like I was helping and needed.

He took my hand as we went out to the garden to pick peas, green beans, and other vegetables. Our water came from a spring below the house. Al would take my hand as we walked and sometimes ran down the hill to the spring to get a bucket of water. He usually seemed to know where I was, so he could know I was safe.

When Al started to high school, he went to live with his grade-school teacher, who lived on a farm close to town, with her husband and two grown daughters. He was to help on the farm to pay for his room and board. Eventually, that didn't work out with the farmer because the teacher and her daughters encouraged Al to get involved in sports and other school activities. He didn't have much time to work on the farm. He quit school and moved into a rented room in town with a friend and worked in a service station. When he turned seventeen years, he joined the Navy.

WW II started. Al was on the USS Wichita Battleship. He saw some of the worst horrors of the war as ships sank around him. He and his shipmates were not allowed to help rescue the sailors in the water. They were on a battleship and could not stop to help. He was in combat at eighteen years of age and for more than three years.

When I was twelve years old, we moved to Winchester, Kansas. No one there knew our family history. One day we got a letter from Al saying he was coming home on leave. When I told my teacher, she asked me if he would talk to the students about the navy. She asked me his name, and I told her his full name. She looked at me curiously, and said, "Is he a half-brother?" I had never heard of a half-brother. I said, "No, he's a whole brother." Even though I knew the older brothers had a different father, we never called them half-brothers.

While in the navy, Al met a lovely young woman, Roberta, in California. They soon fell in love and were married. When he was discharged, he settled into work for the post office in California. He and 'Berta had two daughters. He was a self-taught puppeteer, ventriloquist, and a child evangelist in his spare time. He played guitar and sang, skills he learned back on the farm. Al's daughters sang with him and helped him with his puppets. The girls became so attached to the puppets they claimed them as their brothers.

When Al retired, he and 'Berta traveled throughout the country doing child evangelism with his puppets. A few times, they came to our family reunions, adding much entertainment and fun to the usual crowd of over four hundred family and guests. I feel that he is singing in Heaven now .

I never considered them to be half-brothers: They were always whole brothers in every way.

1925 – Five "Whole" Brothers
Don, Jesse, Lonnie, Francis, Alvin

1938 - Their Dad – Five Brothers – Anna (mother)

FIVE MORE BROTHERS AND 'LIL EARL

When I first counted my brothers, I had ten. Earl, one of a set of twins, would have made eleven living brothers. He died at ten days. We never forgot him, especially his twin brother, Murrel, and Mom and Daddy.

Usually, my other brothers, two older and three younger treated me as "one of the boys." They often pushed and shoved each other, and me, in good-humored, rough-and-tumble play. If I complained, they would call me a "Sissy," so I didn't complain. I wanted to be as tough as they were. It seemed I was just another sibling with no special favors from them. But they wouldn't have let anything or anyone harm me.

JAMES: He was four years older than me. When I was four years old, he started teaching me ABCs and numbers. I learned to say my ABCs, how to write them, and write my name in cursive. I could write numbers and count to one-hundred by "ones" and "twos." The ability to do this put me ahead of the other first-graders.

In school, James was a good student and a good athlete. Daddy taught him carpentry skills, and he did a lot of restoration work on the old Victorian house in Winchester, Kansas, where we lived when he went to high school. Daddy also taught him about gardening and caring for animals. We still had horses and cows, and James helped care for them.

During James' high school years, he worked in our "Victory Garden" during the war and worked for local farmers after school. He graduated from high school on a Sunday and answered his draft call into the army the following Saturday. World War II was ending, but the draft was still in effect.

After basic training, they sent him to Europe for the duration of his time in the army. When James came back, he started to college in Pittsburg, Kansas, close to some of our aunts, uncles, and cousins in Joplin, and Galena, Kansas. After a few semesters, he quit college and worked for a music company giving guitar lessons.

James became acquainted with our nearby relatives, especially a pretty, young girl, Velma. She was the daughter of our first cousin, making her our first cousin once removed. After a couple of years, feeling they were very much in love, they were married. They had two sons about the same age as Bill and my two sons. Not long after they were married, James moved his family to Kansas City, where he went to draftsman school. He worked there for over twenty years, and they had another son. James and Velma eventually divorced.

Several years later, James married Lois, a lovely woman near his age. They have had many good years together. He has kept busy in retirement, doing yard work, and gardening. He has slowed down at this writing but is still with his wife and living a good life.

ROBERT: Bob was two years older than me and helped teach me my ABCs and numbers. He was a good reader and liked to memorize poems. However, he wanted the freedom of the outdoors and soon lost interest in school. He graduated from eighth grade but was not interested in going any further. We lived in Winchester, Kansas then, but he went to Wichita to live with my older brother and get a job that would pay well.

One evening in Wichita, he went to a circus show and was hooked. When he was fifteen years old, he ran away with the circus. We didn't hear from him for over a year. So soon after the war was over, Mom didn't need that worry.

While he was gone, the family moved to Rich Hill, Missouri. One Sunday morning, the phone rang, and it was Bob. He was in Joplin at an aunt's house and wanted us to come and get him. The family loaded in the car and drove the eighty miles to get him, driving about forty miles an hour, the speed limit then. We came back home on the same day.

In Rich Hill, Bob worked with Daddy in his carpentry business. When he turned eighteen, he joined the army, and they sent him to Japan. He was in Japan when Daddy died in a car accident. Somehow the message sent by the Red Cross didn't reach him. He didn't know until several weeks later when he got Mom's letter, telling him how much we missed Daddy. Bob got Mom on his allotment for the rest of the time he was in the army.

After Bob left the army, he went to Wichita to work. He met a pretty, young girl, Donna, and in a few months, they got married. They had four girls and two boys. While in Wichita, he became a Union Iron Worker. After a few years, he moved his family to Defiance, Ohio, where work was plentiful, and wages were good.

When Bob retired and their children grown, he moved close to Springfield, Missouri, to be close to a brother and other family living there. He moved to the country where he could have a big garden. They had all the vegetables they wanted, and he gave the rest to needy people, especially older adults, and the Senior Center. He was a giving person.

Bob also loved fun. He and Donna often traveled to visit their extended family throughout the country. When at home, they spent much time at the Senior Center for dinners and dances. He lived a full life, and all who knew him loved him.

FREDRICK: Fred, or Freddie, was one year and three weeks younger than me. He was my "Little Buddy" on the farm. We spent a lot of time playing together. While trying to be helpful to me, at four years old, he broke my crayons so I would have more. He wasn't rough like the other two brothers. That is until we started growing up. Fred told me that the pushing and shoving we did in good-natured play was as rough as his brothers.

Fred finished eighth grade and quit school. He went to work with Daddy doing carpentry work in Rich Hill. When Daddy went to Kansas City to work, Fred went with him. He was with Daddy when he died in the car accident. When the car rolled, it threw Fred from the front seat into the back seat, and suffered a broken forearm, which went untreated until three weeks later. He did not mention it, and no one noticed it because of all that was happening.

The accident happened at six o'clock in the evening on a rural highway. The car rolled, and it threw Daddy out onto the pavement with an obvious fatal head injury. It was about twenty minutes before anyone drove by and stopped to help. At fifteen and a half years old, Fred was there alone. He has lived with the memory of that horrible experience for the rest of his life.

When Fred was seventeen, he joined the navy during the Korean War. He saw heavy combat and suffered an injury, receiving an early discharge. While in the navy, he started writing to a girl back home that the family knew, named Donna. When he came home, he began dating her, a pretty, young blonde. Before long, they were married and moved to Wichita for better work. They have two sons and one daughter.

Fred spent his working life doing transmission and bodywork on cars with his sons following in his footsteps, and sometimes he followed their work. For years he lived in Colorado and eventually moved to Republic, Missouri, where his brother, Jesse, lived. After many years, he and Donna divorced. He married again but later got divorced.

Fred learned to play the guitar and sing, sort of, when he was in grade school. We felt he had to work at learning the chords and singing on key. As he grew up, he perfected his singing and playing, got a band together, and performed in his spare time, playing evenings and weekends. His sons played and sang with him. made several CDs that sold well.

When Fred partially retired, he continued to work with his sons on auto repair and auto bodywork. But he devoted most of his time to his band that played for dances, especially for seniors. They became well known throughout the area, and they were booked as much as they wanted, providing much pleasure for others.

He is now retired from performing and does occasional auto work. He is well known and has lots of friends. During the season, he spends much of his time gardening. He lives in his own small home, close to his family, children, and grandchildren, and is devoted to them as they are devoted to him.

Freddie is a full-grown man now, but he is still my "Little Buddy."

MURREL: His birth was one of my first memories when I was three years old. As already noted, he was one of a set of twin boys. His twin, Earl, died at ten days.

I recall little about Murrel until he was a few years old. I remember that his speech seemed to be his invention, and he was difficult to understand until he was past three years old. We were concerned that his speech would always be impaired, but it wasn't. It didn't stop him from talking then and for the rest of his life.

I didn't spend much time with Murrel until we moved to Rich Hill when I was fourteen. There was a skating rink, and we both learned to skate. Being about the same size then, we soon realized that we made a good skating pair. Skating together, one trick we "invented" was, with me skating fast backward and Murrel skating fast forward, he leaped as I turned, and he would land, hopefully, on his feet skating backward.

After Mom moved to El Dorado Springs and I stayed in Rich Hill when I was seventeen, I often didn't see Murrel. He started high school and was a good student and an athlete. When he turned sixteen, he quit school to work in a service station to help the family. The family then moved to Wichita, where work opportunities were better. Mom bought an acreage on the west side of Wichita to have a horse and a cow.

Murrel had learned from Daddy how to train horses. There was a local TV star who had a horse show and performed live before the public. As Murrel watched the man, he realized he could train his horse to do more and better tricks. He contacted the man and was soon on TV and had the horse performing tricks. One trick was having the horse lie down beside him. He would put the corner of a blanket in the horse's mouth, and the horse would cover both with the blanket. I saw it myself!

In Wichita, Murrel worked in a service station until he was old enough to work for the railroad. He had a brief marriage that ended in divorce. Later he met and married a lovely young woman named Rita, and together they had a son and a daughter. After a couple of years, the railroad transferred him to Pueblo, Colorado. They drafted him into the army and served the usual time but did not go overseas.

After he left the army, he returned to working for the railroad in Pueblo. He learned of a rancher who owned, trained, and showed horses. Murrel moved to his ranch and worked for him part-time. The man had an Arabian stallion that had been abused before he got him. No one had been able to handle the horse. Murrel got him under control, showing the stallion locally and eventually throughout the country, even Madison Square Gardens, winning many first places.

Murrel was so successful at showing horses that a wealthy Arabian Horse owner in California recruited him to manage his ranch, show his horses and work in his horse breeding business He and Rita moved to California and spent many decades there through good and bad times. He credited Rita with managing the business end of their work and scheduling his appearances. Eventually, however, their marriage ended in divorce.

When Murrel retired, he moved back to Missouri to be closer to siblings. And I felt, to be close to where his twin brother, "Lil Earl," was buried. They would bury him beside Earl. Even though Murrel has departed this life, he left a legacy that lives on.

WALTER: We called him "Walder" when we were kids, then learned to say Walter, then Walt. He was the youngest of the brothers, four-and-a-half years younger than me. He seemed to always be up to mischief. One time I remember, they saw him running fast toward the barn. Mom called him back, and it was easy to see why. He had gotten hold of Daddy's hand clippers and cut an inch-wide swath out of the front of his hair.

We left the farm when Walt was in first grade, which was difficult for him. His first-grade teacher in the Joplin schools scolded and punished him for spelling his last name "Lacey" instead of "Lacy." We moved three times during his first two years of school. After three more moves, he finished high school, the last one in Wichita, where he graduated. He was only the second of the brothers to finish high school.

He didn't especially like going to church and only attended when made to go. He attended church, at Mom's request, on his twenty-first birthday and decided to follow Christ. He became active in a church in Wichita and felt a calling to the ministry.

One summer, a group of young missionaries visited Walt's church for a few days, and one young woman caught his attention. She was a lovely young woman named Gail. Because she was a missionary, she could not date. Walt said he attempted to keep in contact with her through friends and letters.

Having decided to become a minister, Walt wanted to start o college. With the draft still in effect, he enlisted in the army while in college. They sent him to Germany for eighteen months. He convinced Gail to correspond with him. Upon his discharge from the army, they dated for a few months and were eventually married. They have a daughter and a son.

Walt went to college and seminary in Texas. He moved his family to California, where he obtained his Master's Degree and Doctorate in the Ministry. He pastored churches there for many years before moving back near Kansas City to pastor a church there for several years. When he left the ministry, he developed a consulting firm, doing management seminars for churches and businesses throughout the United States and seventeen countries.

He is now retired, somewhat, but does interim pastoring in local churches and has done substitute teaching in local high schools. Gail gives piano lessons, and they have a full life with their friends and family, especially the grandchildren.

The difference between my older brothers and my younger brothers is clear-cut. My older brothers sheltered and protected me, maybe even spoiled me. In contrast, my younger brothers may have shown me how to take life's punches without complaining and eventually defend myself. Both were a good preparation for life—I think.

I have written only briefly of my five other brothers. It would take volumes to cover their adventures, escapades, successes, failures, and who knows what else. I'll leave it to them to write their own story.

Herb, Anna, Bonnie, and five brothers - 1938

Bonnie and all ten brothers - 1938

THIS OLD HOUSE

W hy does the faded picture of the old house hold such attraction for me? It is the first house I remember. I was four years old when Daddy and my brothers built it.

The ritual of putting up the stove-pipe chimney as shown in the picture happened each fall. Mom didn't want the heating stove in the small front room until late in the fall and it had to be it taken out early in the spring. A visitor with his camera, who thought the procedure quaint took the picture. We didn't have a camera. He did not intend to take a picture of the house, but there it stands, stark and weathered.

Daddy is standing facing the house directing my brother and a cousin how to secure the stove-pipe chimney. The barren trees in the background are a stark reminder of the time of year. When it got cold, before the stove was in place, Mom and I would shiver in our long underwear, which we slept in, by the warm kitchen stove until we could get dressed in the morning. The guys were tougher and dressed in their rooms.

They finished the house in early spring, from freshly sawed lumber on the farm, so we could move in time to plant spring crops. Daddy planned to build our "Dream House" later, from cured native lumber on the farm. Because of hard times during the Depression, he could never build it.

The freshly sawed lumber of the house shrank as it seasoned and cured. After a few months, the narrow lateral strips warped as they cured and left cracks between the boards where the wind blew in. Mom tore long strips of fabric and we stuffed them in the cracks to keep the wind out. There were no inside walls.

Mom and Daddy struggled to make a living, but they never lost hope. They never quit, and they never gave up. Life lessons taught and learned by my brothers and me. We had what we needed, but there were few extras. We laughed at each other, with each other and, at ourselves. We seldom spoke of love, sometimes not recognizing it. But it was there, binding us together.

There was sickness and there was sadness. There was anger, too, chronic, unresolved anger. Most often, though, frequent flareups were resolved and forgotten. There were many fun times when neighbors gathered at our house for parties. I remember the old house as a place of fun, security and comfort. It became our home.

It had no electricity and no indoor plumbing, only a well for water and an outhouse. We had no radio or car. So, what was there? There was always enough food because Daddy and the boys planted a great variety of crops. He often shared food with our neighbors. Mom's cooking and having milk and eggs made the variety of foods grown better.

There were fun times close by the old house. We had horses for working and going places by team and wagon and for the boys to ride for fun. They often rode the cows and pigs when Daddy wasn't watching. Down the hillside, there was a creek with a swimming hole and lots of catfish. And there were hickory, walnut and sycamore trees for the boys to climb and have fun swinging back and forth on. I didn't join in that game.

But I learned to swim and ride horses. My favorite

pastime was wandering around in the woods, close to the house, and picking greens for Mom to cook. I also picked wildflowers for her, which made her smile.

My baby sister, my only sister, and another brother were born in the house, two girls and ten boys in our family. We never, though, forgot Little Earl. One of a set of twins, he died at ten days when I was three years old. He made eleven brothers.

We lived in the old house from the time I was four years old until I was ten. Those six years there molded my life. Those formative years taught me to be strong and tough. And to love, no matter the circumstances. The great and valuable life lessons I learned then have stayed with me the rest of my life.

I often wander back in my memories to those happy times when I was a little girl and life was so simple for me. I did not know there was any other way to live.

Over our life together, Bill and I had five houses, our homes. Two of them were nearly new. He humored me by reluctantly agreeing to buy two Victorian houses that needed restoring, otherwise we could not have afforded them. Bill didn't understand my fascination for ornate and decorative old houses. He never saw the house or the pictures of "This Old House!"

"This Old House" - 1935

Gathering in 1935
All the family, except Walter

LIVING

Trees and grass and fields of wildflowers.
Playing and sleeping.
Mom cooking:
Eggs, milk, biscuits, molasses, gravy, cracklins,
greens, mushrooms.

Brothers everywhere; pampering, disciplining and teasing.
Daddy was sick; he couldn't hold me.
The doctor came; Daddy had blood poisoning, fever.
The days were hot, and the nights.
The neighbors stood over Daddy fanning, day and night.
July, '34; Missouri, misery.

The doctor came.
My brothers said Mom was tired; she couldn't hold me.
The doctor picked me up and told me
I had two new baby brothers.
I already had brothers of every size.
A baby brother, brothers about my size
and big brothers like Daddy.

Hot; no rain, only hot days and nights
and fussy, crying babies.
The neighbors stood over them and Mom,
fanning day and night.

The doctor came; he left quietly.
The neighbors were there, quiet and unsmiling.
Grandpa said the baby had gone to Heaven
to be with God.
But Daddy built a box and they put him in the ground.
The man in strange clothes said
the baby's spirit was in Heaven.

I hoped my spirit didn't go to Heaven.
I was barely three.

The rains came!
We had to shoo the chickens inside so they wouldn't drown.
They didn't know what rain was.
Now the chickens would lay eggs again,
the cows would give milk again.

We romped and splashed and played in the rain.
Too late, the rain, for Spring and Summer crops;
they never came up.
Daddy and my brothers planted acres of turnips;
they grew fast.
We ate turnips and all the animals ate turnips.
The cow's milk tasted like turnips,
the sausage tasted like turnips.

Winter winds same through the wooden floors
and around the doors and windows.

Mom and Daddy slept with my little brother
and the baby and me.

To keep us warm, because the wood fires went out at night.
Also, to keep us protected from the rats.

Spring! Everything in the house was loaded on the wagon;
we had no car.
Daddy and my big brothers were building a new home.
Made from trees they cut and sawed at the saw mill.
Just framework and boxing; he'd build a better one later.
They had to hurry and plant spring crops.
Days of hard work and play; our own swimming hole.
Nights of fun, laughter and singing,
from somewhere a guitar.
Acres of trees: walnut, persimmon, sycamore,
hickory and pawpaw.

Blackberries by the tub full, watermelon, tomatoes,
potatoes and corn.
The first fruits and vegetables I could remember.
Now we had enough to eat.

Mom was tired; my brothers helped her in the kitchen.
The doctor came, carrying his black bag.
My brothers told me doctors don't bring babies, and why.
The new baby was a boy; now there were ten brothers.
One girl; I was four years old.

Winter winds whistled through the wooden floors
and through the boxing.
At night we snuggled together in beds to keep warm.
Somewhat contented, lots of love, nobody sick.

Spring!
My brothers went swimming on Easter Sunday, always.
Even if they had to break the skifts of ice on the swimming
hole.
Daddy went to town to get seeds; horseback,
we had no car.
Someday I would get to go to town where big people go.
We made a garden, barefoot; everyone worked and played.

School!
Finally! I get to go to school where my brothers go.
The first special thing that ever happened to me.

New crayons for me, my own tablet and pencil!
Mom made me a new chambray dress.
My big brother carried me the two miles on his back.
Those girls in frilly dresses, blonde curls, blue eyes
and pink skin.
I didn't look like other girls look!

With straight bobbed, brown hair, dark eyes,
dark, tanned skin; and barefoot.
Girls play different games than boys:
jacks, hopscotch, jump rope.
So many things to see: a bicycle, a piano, jello,
the teacher's car.
Books about strange people that were a different color
than I was.
Books about lands far away.

They started Church in the schoolhouse on Sunday.
I had never heard of church; the family went in the wagon.
The preacher said we should love thy neighbor as thyself.
Strange; I had never heard of that.
He gave me a little Bible.
I learned to read; the first chapter of Genesis.
Now I knew most everything; I was almost nine.

Spring came.
Mom was tired, in bed; my brother helped
with the cooking and homework.
My big brother woke me one morning.
He said we had a new baby sister; he couldn't fool me!
I ran to Mom, who was still in bed.
She showed me; the baby was a girl!
My world was complete; what more could I want.

War! What was that?
Handsome brothers in uniform, going off to protect us,
Mom said.
Five of them! But they could die!
Hadn't Grandma died?
She was grouchy, didn't like little kids,
and smoked a smelly pipe.
I tried to cry when she died, because Daddy was crying,
but I couldn't.

How I prayed for my brothers,
though I wasn't sure how to pray.
Night after night, year after year, always remembering.
They all came back! Had God really heard?

Daddy worked building defense plants during the war;
we moved many times.
Now that the war was over, we could stay in one place.
I could go to one school; I was fourteen.

I was no longer mistaken for one of the boys;
that was nice.
It had been fun to be a tomboy or a girl, as I chose.
It was good to be almost a woman.
I had become somebody special in school;
good grades, good in sports.
I was outstanding for the first time; it felt good.

Jesus became real to me!
A peace and joy I had never known before!

Daddy. They said he died instantly in the car wreck.
He was so special to me.
He taught me to hope and dream.
I was sixteen.

I didn't want a boyfriend; I had heard my brothers
talk about girls!
Bill! He would be a friend; the best friend I could ever have.
I was sixteen! What was happening?
It was good to be a woman.
I was eighteen; we were married.
Bill, my best friend, my lover, the father of my children.
Two sons and two daughters, in that order, in four years.
Time moves so fast!

War again! What kind of war is this?
A son AWOL? It may be said, "The enemy is us."
How brave he was to stand by his convictions!
Another son saved by the lottery.
Both now safe! But what of all the other wasted lives?
"The enemy is us!"

Can it be; our little girls have grown up?
Just yesterday I was braiding their pigtails.

Mom, the tiny matriarch! She has gone to be with her Jesus!
She taught me to have compassion for others.
So much of her is still with me; I shall always miss her.

What? I'm a grandmother?
*But grandmothers are old and grouchy and strange; not this
one!*
I am a woman, a daughter, a mother, a sister, a scholar!
I am a wife, a friend and a lover.
For Bill and me, life is good; most of it is still ahead of us!

Bonnie Lacey Krenning
June 1975

OUR FIRST CHRISTMAS TREE

One precious memory of my childhood is our family's first Christmas tree. I had never seen or heard of Christmas trees when I started to the one-room country school at age five. Families didn't have them in their homes; only churches, schools, and stores had them.

As the Christmas season came near, the older boys in our school cut a cedar tree from an adjoining pasture with the farmer's permission. When I saw the teacher's pretty decorations and the pretty decorations the kids made and put on the tree, I wished we could have a Christmas tree.

That night I asked Daddy if we could have a Christmas tree. He just smiled but didn't answer. Later I saw him whispering to Mom.

The next Saturday afternoon, Daddy told me to put on my coat stocking cap. He lifted me on his shoulders and carried me out to the pasture and set me down. He cut a cedar tree as tall as he was. When we got home, he made a stand for the tree and set it in the corner of the front room.

Mom popped lots of popcorn. My brothers and I strung it on a string, made long ropes, and draped them around the tree. We hung stars and snowflakes, cut from white paper. And we made colorful paper chain ropes from strips we colored on tablet paper. They all looked so pretty on the dark green tree.

We had no icicles, but Daddy took care of that. One day he brought home a small roll of lead foil from the ignition system of an old car someone gave him. We carefully cut the foil into thin strips and draped them on the tree branches. They were so pretty at night in the lamplight. We were the only family in the neighborhood that had a Christmas tree at home.

I have had many Christmas trees. But in my memory, it still seems like that first tree was the most beautiful Christmas tree ever!

MOM ON THE FARM

When I first became aware of daily life on the farm, I was four years old. It seemed Mom was always in the kitchen cooking. She didn't sit down, except for our meals and in the evening with the family. In the early morning, as I came into the kitchen, she was standing by the large, ornate, wood-burning cookstove, cooking breakfast.

Close by was the kitchen cupboard, where she kept her needed supplies to cook three meals a day for our large family. Starting from scratch on the cupboard's work-surface, she made biscuits, cornbread, sourdough bread, pie crusts, dumplings, and noodles, to mention just a few. To this day, I can remember the smells that filled the house.

Mom was particular about the kinds and cuts of wood she needed and wanted for the cookstove. Daddy and the boys made sure she had them. There was kindling, split and dry wood, and small green logs in wood boxes behind the cookstove to keep the heat at the temperature she needed as she cooked different foods and bread. Even with a broken thermometer on the oven door, she could control the fire, so everything turned out perfectly baked and cooked.

We always had a big early breakfast. While Daddy and the boys were out at the barn feeding the animals and milking the cows, Mom was cooking. She cooked various breakfasts such as biscuits and gravy, rolled oats, rice, eggs, and biscuits. On rare occasions, she fried stacks of large, plate-size pancakes. Starting with two stacks of pancakes, each six to eight inches high, she continued frying until all of us had all we wanted. That meant she made a lot of pancakes.

Without fail, every Monday, Wednesday, and Friday morning, Mom started a big batch of sourdough bread from the starter she kept active in a gallon crock. She mixed flour and liquid into the dough until she could knead it and let it rise. As the dough raised to nearly overflowing the dishpan, she kneaded it several times during the day so it would be light and fine-textured. She made six large loaves of bread in pans of three loaves each and let them rise double for baking about mid-afternoon. There was enough dough for a large pan of cinnamon rolls, a family favorite.

The yeast bread was not enough to last from one yeast bread day until the next, so Mom made cornbread, biscuits, pancakes, and sometimes cornmeal mush—called grits in the south. And for several weeks in the spring, delicious Morel Mushrooms grew down by the creek. She sliced and fried them for breakfast, two or three times a week for several weeks. They made a complete meal and were so delicious.

Anna Mae Stroer—best known as "Mom" to me, and "Annie Mae" to Daddy—was known throughout the neighborhood for her great cooking and fine bread. I remember how occasionally one of our neighbors would just happen by at mealtime, hoping to enjoy her cooking. The family welcomed them. There was always plenty of food, even if sometimes there was not much variety, especially in the wintertime.

The family appreciated Mom's cooking but rarely told her. One day in winter, after the noon meal, the boys had finished eating and left the table to run out to play. It was before spring crops came in, so Mom "made do" with whatever she had on hand, probably some kind of beans and cornbread and maybe a fruit cobbler. I was clearing the table while Daddy was drinking his coffee. Mom was sitting close by. I heard Daddy quietly say to Mom, "Annie Mae, you can take almost anything and make it taste good, better than anyone I know." And she could!

Throughout spring and summer, Mom cooked fresh vegetables from the garden every day. She had the cookstove fire going all day, even when the outside temperature was over 100 degrees. In the kitchen, the temperature was over 110 degrees. There were no fans and seldom a breeze through the screen doors. Her hair and clothes were often wet with sweat, which she wiped away with a "kerchief" she kept in her apron pocket. She just kept on working, didn't complain.

That summer, I noticed Mom going barefoot like the rest of us. When I asked her why, she said, "To save my nice shoes." Her only pair of shoes had high heels. They hurt her feet and the corns on her toes from wearing shoes that didn't fit. The rare times she bought shoes, they told her that her feet were short and wide, and she was fit accordingly. Many years later, she found that her correct shoe size was a 7A. The wrong shoe size caused the corns and callouses. Even with the pain, she always kept her shoes close at hand, in case a neighbor stopped by so she wouldn't be seen barefoot by an outsider.

To me, Mom was beautiful, even when she was barefoot. She had dark brown eyes and beautiful, long black hair that she kept pulled back in a neat bun. When she sat down in the evening and let her thick hair down, it was long enough for her to sit on. I loved combing it. My hair was fine and thin and never grew long. I remember wishing my hair was pretty like hers.

Mom was five feet, two inches tall, and weighed about 120 pounds when she wasn't having a baby. I recall she was always neat and clean. She wore a cotton print dress and an apron, which she quickly removed if someone stopped by. She ironed our dresses with a flat iron heated on the cookstove. Some neighbor women sometimes wore wrinkled dresses and often didn't look clean. But some women had to work in the gardens and fields. With all my brothers, Mom didn't have to do that. I remember her telling me that she felt it was just as important to look nice at home as when you went somewhere.

Most of Mom's and my dresses, except the hand-me-downs, were made from printed feed sacks on her treadle sewing machine. She had a "fancy dress" that hung in the closet, by Daddy's dress suit, that she wore on special occasions.

I loved being around Mom and listening to her singing in a beautiful, clear soprano voice. She sang hymns, Jimmy Rogers songs, and folk and mountain ballads. She learned the songs in better times before the Depression and before moving to the farm. She knew the words to many songs and liked it when we asked her to sing one of our favorites.

Through it all, I don't remember Mom being sad or depressed. However, in the wintertime, she would sometimes say, "I wish it wus summer agin!" And in the summertime, she would say, "I wish it wus winter agin!" It is easy to understand her feelings with it being stifling hot in the summertime. Then in winter, it was so cold, with the cold winds blowing around the windows and doors that she wore her ill-fitting shoes. And, more than once, the water in the bucket in the kitchen froze solid overnight.

The boys took turns helping Mom in the kitchen. She seldom raised her voice, but she didn't have to. Everyone knew what they were supposed to do and usually did it. When she said, "Bonnie Mae," I knew I had better do what I was supposed to do or stop doing what I wasn't supposed to do, or she would "raise her voice" to me.

I can recall the first and only time when Mom physically punished me. Whether it was something I didn't do that I was supposed to do or something I did that I shouldn't have done, I don't remember. She said, "Yer gonna have to have a switchin! Go git me a switch!" I went outside and got the thinnest switch I could find and brought it back to her in the kitchen.

Mom stood beside me and pulled my dress tight against my bloomers and lightly switched me a few times. It didn't really hurt, but I thought it was such an indignity, so I threw myself down on the floor, sobbing. She kept lightly switching me, saying, "Git up! Git up!" So, I quickly got up, and it was all over. It never happened again. I don't know whether I learned my lesson or whether Mom was simply not inclined to repeat the "switchin'."

Our family worked as a team, and Mom was in charge, clearly leading the way, especially on wash day. Washday was always on Saturday so the boys could help. They carried many two-gallon buckets of water from the spring below the house and built a fire outside under our large cast-iron kettle to heat the water. They poured the hot water into two washtubs on the ground and added lye soap that Mom and Daddy made. In cold weather, we placed the washtubs inside on the kitchen floor. They put several pairs of overalls and other heavily soiled clothes in the tubs and left them to soak.

When the water cooled enough, we smaller barefoot kids would step into the tubs and "stomp" the clothes to get out the worst of the dirt. The boys wore their overalls for a week at a time, so they were really dirty. The overalls were wrung out by hand by the boys working two together. They transferred the overalls to washtubs of warm water on benches in the kitchen. Mom and the older boys did the final scrubbing on washboards. After rinsing the overalls, the boys hung them on the clothesline to dry.

Washday in the summertime was usually a fun time for my brothers and me. The boys went without shirts and underwear in the summer, so there were fewer clothes to wash. But in the wintertime, all the washing was done in the kitchen, and they hung the clothes out to freeze dry or draped them on chairs around the heating stoves in the front room and dining room to dry.

Sometimes it was just too cold to do the washing. Then we would have to wear the same long underwear and outer clothes for two or three weeks.

Fortunately, or maybe unfortunately, most of the neighborhood families went without washing clothes as our family did, so we probably all "smelled" about the same.

The biggest problem may have been in the one-room schoolhouse. It was not easy, though, to keep the room warm, because there was only a wood- burning heating stove in the middle of the large classroom. The room was often cool, even cold. The younger kids sat closer to the stove, and the older boys sat farther away. That may have helped to lessen the "aroma."

About two years before we left the farm, Daddy bargained for a used washing machine with a gas-powered motor. It had a wringer, and two wooden tubs meant for washing and rinsing the clothes. We didn't have to, or maybe get to, "stomp" the clothes anymore with the washing machine. The washing machine completely changed and improved Mom's life.

Every fall, for several evenings, the family gathered around the dining table. Not to eat, but to help Mom make our denim quilts that were so essential for us to keep warm when the fires burned down at night in the wintertime. She didn't have time to do "fancy" quilting, but she had a few nice quilts she used on her and Daddy's bed.

When the boys' overalls were completely worn out, Mom cut squares of fabric from the legs' backs and sewed them together to make a denim quilt top. She bought dark flannel by the bolt, thirty-six inches wide, and sewed two long strips together to make the outer lining for a quilt. She spread it out on the dining table and placed an old worn sheet blanket on the lining and a denim top placed on it. Sometimes she covered a worn-out denim quilt with new flannel outer lining and a "new" denim top, making a "new quilt." They became quite thick and heavy; that was good!

The older boys tacked through the quilt every few inches with a darning needle and string. They cut the string between where they tacked the quilt, and the younger kids tied the string in hard knots to hold it together. Mom sewed the outer edges together all around the quilt at another time. We made and covered several quilts each fall.

In the coldest weather, we had to cover ourselves with layers of quilts to keep warm when the temperature dropped below freezing in the house at night. The boys could snuggle together, but I slept alone.

Sometimes Mom wrapped a warm lid from the cookstove in newspaper and put it at my feet to help keep me warm. I would often wake up shivering, realizing I had wet the bed. I didn't want anyone to know because Mom would call me "a peetail." But she found out anyway in the morning when she took the cookstove lid out of my bed.

Mom spent many evenings patching the boys' and Daddy's overalls. She sometimes sewed patches on patches on their overalls, and they got handed down to a younger brother. Daddy and the boys each had a good pair of overalls to wear places away from home. Daddy watched the boys to make sure they changed into work overalls when they got home. Patching overalls was a difficult task, but Mom felt it was important, even necessary. It saved a lot of money that could be used for other necessities. Also, she would never have allowed the boys or Daddy to wear "ragged" clothes.

When the long winter was over, the wonder of spring took hold on all of us. Trees started to blossom and leaf out. Daddy and the boys planted the garden and fields. Before that, the mushrooms, wild greens, and wild onions grew big enough to eat. We went all winter with no fresh vegetables or fruit. We did well on beans, grains, potatoes, home-canned berries, sauerkraut, and many kinds of pickles. We had enough to eat but longed for fresh foods.

The spring I turned five years old, I started noticing Mom as she worked. I wanted to learn to do the things she did so I could help her. I was usually at her elbow, watching and trying to help. She was so patient with me and showed me how to do many tasks. I learned how to peel potatoes, pick, and shell green peas, pick and snap green beans, shuck the ears of corn, and cut and wash the asparagus. Sometimes these tasks took me two or three hours, but I was pleased to be helping Mom, and we were all happy to have all the fresh vegetables we wanted.

The only thing Mom took charge of outside the house was the chickens. She counted on eggs often for breakfast and cooking, to make the noodles, dumplings, cakes, puddings, chocolate meringue pies, and other foods that called for eggs.

She had Plymouth Rock hens and roosters because they were larger and produced more eggs than other breeds. We had a chicken house where the nests were about four feet off the ground, so the blacksnakes could not easily reach the eggs and swallow them whole. Occasionally a snake got into a nest and swallowed an egg. Sometimes we saw a snake crawling on the ground with a bulge that showed it had eaten an egg. Mom hated blacksnakes. She kept a hoe by the kitchen door, and if the boys told her they saw a blacksnake, she would take the hoe and chase it down and cut off its head.

In the spring, when nesting season started, some hens sat on nests in the chicken house and hatched their baby chicks. Some hens would go into the woods, make a nest, lay and hatch the eggs. The hens and chicks would then come into the yard for the grains we scattered for the new chicks.

When the chicks were grown, they kept the hens for layers, to keep the flock going. They kept some of the roosters for mating, and they used the others for chicken and noodles and chicken and dumplings in the fall. Chickens were our main source of meat.

Each spring, Mom ordered two boxes of one-hundred baby chicks from a hatchery in town, one box at a time. She mailed cash in an envelope to the hatchery, and the mailman brought baby chicks to our mailbox. One of my brothers would go to the mailbox every day until the mailman delivered the chicks. He carried the baby chicks the quarter mile to the house. They were raised for fryers for the family or trade at the country store to exchange for needed groceries.

One summer morning, a magazine salesman came walking up the hill to our house unexpectedly. Mom told him that she didn't have any money for magazines. When he saw all the chickens running around, he offered to sell Mom magazines in exchange for chickens. She ordered a year's subscription to *The Lady's Home Journal* and *Good Housekeeping* for her and the *Jack and Jill Magazine* for us kids. She traded four fryers for all the magazines.

With the coming of summer, Mom started preparing food from the garden for the winter. She didn't have a pressure cooker, so she canned only acid foods. I picked the gooseberries, and the boys picked the blackberries. I had buckets of gooseberries, but the boys picked washtubs full of blackberries. She canned over a hundred half-gallon jars of berries to make several berry cobblers throughout the winter months.

Mom made five-gallon crocks of sauerkraut, beet pickles, and cucumber pickles. She seasoned them and knew just when they were ready, to heat and can in half-gallon jars. Along with the sweet potatoes and red-skinned potatoes, we were all set for winter. When freezing weather came, the canned food and potatoes had to be stored in Daddy's root cellar to keep them from freezing.

My mom loved black walnuts. She considered them one of our most important crops. She used them in her baking, but just as importantly, she crushed the nutmeats and squeezed the oil out into small jars for ear drops to treat our earaches in the wintertime. She believed the oil worked better than anything she could buy at the drug store. Mom relied on "folk medicine" and experience, but she was right. Black walnuts are anti-fungal and have many other health and nutrition benefits.

Every fall, the boys gathered bushel baskets of black walnuts, hulled them, and set them beside a big rock where I cracked them. Cracking the walnuts was my chore, but I loved it. I cracked them and dug the nutmeats out with a hairpin, collecting them in jars. It took several weeks to fill several half-gallon jars with nutmeats for Mom to use in the desserts she made.

She liked doing fun things. It seemed like she even enjoyed her work. She enjoyed having neighbor families in to pop popcorn and make popcorn balls. She l laughed and smiled at our family's dancing at home in the winter evenings. And she liked the neighborhood dances. Mom and Daddy did the square dances, waltzes, and two-steps together.

Mom knew all the dances. She and her friend Goldie, the woman that delivered me, liked to do the "Schottische Dance." They danced arm-in-arm across the floor to any peppy tune. Everyone else would step back and clap their hands in time to the music while they danced. Mom was one of the best dancers in the neighborhood.

Women and girls in the neighborhood were not supposed to wear slacks, pants, or Heaven forbid shorts. One day a package came in the mail from one of Daddy's sisters in the city. Mom opened it, and there was a yellow linen slack suit for women. She put it on. It fit perfectly, and she looked so pretty. Daddy smiled his usual big smile of approval, but Mom knew she wouldn't be wearing the suit anywhere off the farm.

One fall day after Sunday dinner, Daddy said to Mom, "If you put on that slack suit, we'll take a walk around on the farm." With Mom in her yellow linen slack suit and Daddy in his best shirt and overalls, they walked off hand-in-hand, out of sight of us kids for a couple of hours.

When they came back, they were talking, smiling, and laughing between themselves. I don't recall seeing the slack suit again, but that one time was worth it all.

Although Mom didn't have much time to read, she enjoyed reading her magazines, the local newspaper, and *The*

Weekly Kansas City Star. Mom and Daddy often discussed the world, national, and local news, including politics. The older boys checked out books at school for them and for Daddy and Mom to read. They liked Harold Bell Wright's books, westerns, and historical novels. Mom had more time to read in the winter when we were in school, and the canning season was over.

Mom was adamant about voting. She was twenty-four years old when women won the right to vote. She believed everyone should vote in all the elections: National, State, and Local. Daddy made sure that she had a ride to the polls. She would have probably walked, but he wouldn't have allowed that.

So that Mom didn't need to walk, Daddy traded for a beautiful old one-horse buggy with a fancy top. It was not big enough for all the family, so they used it when Mom and Daddy went somewhere by themselves and sometimes with little ones. When not in use, the buggy sat idly by the garden fence and was much admired by our visitors. It gave her a chance to let people know she always voted. I don't recall the folks ever missing a chance to vote. I remember one time when they went in the buggy in heavy snow to the schoolhouse to vote.

I learned early not to ask too many questions, so I usually tried to figure things out for myself. One night in late winter, I had been sound asleep but woke up to Mom and Daddy talking in the front room. I kept quiet and listened. I heard Mom say, "We don't have any money. What are we going' to do?" I got up and went into where she was standing by the stove and put my arm around her because she looked sad. She hugged me and told me to go back to bed.

I woke up the next morning, thinking about what she said. I knew that Mom kept her coin purse in her envelope purse. I opened it and saw there were three pennies in it. I didn't tell Mom I had checked but wondered why she said she didn't have any money. Not knowing the value of money, I didn't understand. I thought maybe she didn't know the pennies were there, but I didn't dare say anything.

I checked her coin purse every few days without her knowing, and the pennies were still there. As winter faded into spring, everyone seemed happy and excited about the warmer weather. Then one day, I checked Mom's coin purse, and there were some nickels and dimes in it. Now, Mom wouldn't have to be sad anymore like she was that winter night.

I had not heard of slaves or people with different colored skin in that remote area, except my little negro doll. One day I heard one of my brothers telling Mom that one boy at school said, "Slave mothers didn't care if their babies and children were sold. It's just like Daddy selling our horses and cows." Mom became really upset and started crying. She said, "Don't ever believe that! They love their children just like I love you!"

I didn't realize the full meaning of slavery then but later became aware that neither Mom nor Daddy was prejudiced, unlike many people in the community and the county. There was a sign on 54 Highway, just outside our town that said, "NO NEGROS ALLOWED IN TOWN AFTER SUNDOWN." The sign was not removed until 1948.

In the late 1930s, the country was recovering from the Depression. Markets were up, and the economy was getting better, so there was money for some extras. But I didn't like it when Mom had her beautiful hair cut and got a perm. She said she paid for it by selling some eggs and chickens. She decided I should have a perm in my straight hair, so she saved $2.00 from selling eggs for my perm. Mom's hair turned out nice, but I hated my curly, frizzy hair and was glad when my perm grew out.

I didn't realize it at the time, but I led a very sheltered and protected life in my early childhood. Since I was the only girl among ten brothers until was nine years old, I got a lot of attention Often visitors would give me, just me, a nickel or a few pennies. I could see that Mom didn't want that to happen and was sometimes able to intervene.

I didn't have any way to spend the money, so I would save it until there was enough to give Daddy to buy a large bag of candy for all of us. Then there was the time I saved a few coins and gave it to my brother to buy firecrackers. He bought several little Lady Fingers packages, enough for all of us to have a good time on the Fourth of July.

Mom taught me some pretty songs and poems she learned when she was a little girl in school. They were teaching songs and poems. She didn't want me to be "Tryin' to be fancy." Most of them I have forgotten, but one poem she taught me was to let me know God made me, and I was where I was meant to be. I still remember the poem:

DISCONTENT

Down in the field one day in June the flowers all bloomed
together
Except one who tried to hide herself and drooped that
pleasant weather.
A robin that had flown too high and felt a little lazy
Was resting near a buttercup who wished she were a daisy.
For daisies grow so trim and tall and always have a passion
For wearing frills about their neck in just the daisy fashion.
"You silly thing" the robin said, I think you must be crazy!
I'd rather be my honest self than any made-up daisy."
"Look bravely up into the sky and be content with knowing

That God wished for a buttercup just here where you are
growing."
Author: Sarah Orne Jewett (Excerpt Mom taught me
from a longer poem).

I am blessed to have had such a firm but loving mom
in my early years. She tried to keep me humble. She would
say, "You're no better than anyone else." In the same breath
she would say: "And, nobody else is better than you." I
believed Mom.

Herb and Anna Mae Lacey, 1926

Anna Mae on donkey, age 30

Anna Mae Lacey, age 44

MY ONLY SISTER

All my many brothers have been special to me over the years. Carol Marie has been special and more, a blessing since her birth.

Carol was born when I was nine years old, the last child in our family. Mom was forty-three years young.

June 10, 1940 was one of the most important and memorable days of my life. At that time, I had ten living brothers and no sisters. That spring and summer, I noticed Mom was getting heavier under her loose-fitting dresses. My brothers helped her more often in the kitchen and sometimes whispered with her so I couldn't hear.

One evening Mom said I was going to my aunt's house to spend the night. That was unusual, but I didn't ask any questions. An older brother took me by horseback through the woods to her house, about a mile away, then he went back home. My aunt and I ate supper and went to bed.

The next morning my brother woke me up. He said we had a new baby sister. I didn't know that Mom was getting another baby and didn't believe that the baby could be a girl. We rode horseback through the woods to our house.

Jumping down from the saddle, I ran inside to Mom's bedroom. She was in bed with the new baby sleeping by her side. The baby was so pretty, and so was Mom, smiling and looking happy. I asked her if the baby was a girl, and she said, "Yes." After having all those brothers, I didn't know whether a girl was possible.

I stayed with them until Mom breastfed the baby, and then she started to change the baby's diaper. I watched until I saw that the baby was like me, not like my brothers. Finally, I knew I had a sister. Mom named her Carol Marie.

Mom couldn't continue breastfeeding, so I started giving Carol her bottle. I was soon changing her diaper. When I saw Mom holding and carrying Carol on the side of her hip while she was trying to cook, I asked to hold the baby for her. She had watched me and knew I could hold her safely. Soon I was caring for Carol most of the time.

I carried Baby Carol around almost everywhere I went. She didn't learn to walk as soon as usual. However, she did learn to talk early and a lot and is still talking a lot. She was a little bit spoiled. I did anything she wanted, which I could give her or do for her. I finally had my sister, and Mom had her baby girl.

As she grew, I sewed Carol dresses and dressed her. We walked to school and church together, and I usually took her skating with me.

The summer before my senior high school year, Mom moved to El Dorado Springs. I finished high school in Rich Hill. Carol and I weren't together very often as she grew up.

The summer Carol was turning fourteen on June 10, Bill and I were going to have our fourth child about that time. I had a C-Section and chose that day. Carol spent the summer with us in Kirksville, Missouri, and was a lot of help with the little ones.

In the spring of her junior year in high school, Carol met Jim, who was visiting in her Wichita church. He was a Marine on leave from San Diego and soon returned to the base. Before starting her senior year of high school, Carol spent the summer with us in Kirksville.

Jim and Carol wrote to each other after they met and decided to get married after high school. She went to California, where they married and later had a daughter. They transferred him to Camp Lejeune, N.C. Their family grew, and eventually, they had three beautiful daughters.

Bill and I moved our family to Wichita. Jim was transferred there and worked as a recruiting officer for the Marines. While they lived there, Carol and I spent a lot of time together with our families. Jim coached our boys' church baseball team when they were in their early teens. They respected, admired, and, yes, loved Jim.

But the Marines transferred him to a different base, and after a few years, their marriage failed.

Eventually, Carol met and married Mel. He came from California to buy and start a dairy farm in Missouri. They moved to the farm and added a son, Mark, to their family. Unfortunately, after several years the farm didn't work out. Neither did the marriage, but Mark was a blessing and still is.

Carol started working again and quickly moved into management positions. Free to travel with the companies she was with, she worked in several states, before settling at the Space Center in Florida. While there, she observed space launches. After many years, she retired to North Carolina from the Space Center and then to California, where her oldest daughter lived.

I visited Carol when she lived in North Carolina and attended her daughter's wedding, which took place on a hot air balloon. I was also on the balloon. Carol visited me in Wichita a few years ago, but we didn't repeat the balloon adventure. We keep in contact, sometimes by text, but more often by long phone calls.

Carol is still walking and talking as much, or maybe more than ever. She is still a Blessing to me.

Carol Lacey, age 5

Carol and Bonnie, 2015

TALKIN' PROPER

The new experience of starting to the one-room country school scared and excited me. I was five years old, a year earlier than normal. Some students were as big as men and women. Having moved there less than a year before, some kids didn't know that there was a girl in our family of ten boys, with four in school. It seemed everyone looked out for me.

I soon noticed that the teacher talked so pretty and used words that I had never heard before. She said *isn't* instead of *ain't*, *potatoes* instead of *'taters*, and *tomatoes* instead of *'maters*. There were also many other new words. I soon tried to talk like the teacher.

Talking like her annoyed my brother Bob, two years older than I, and he sometimes acted like he had the right to manage me. He would say, "Quit tryin' to be so proper!" At home, when he heard me trying to talk like my teacher, he would grab me by my forearm and pull me, resisting, to where Mom worked. He would say, "Mom! Bonnie's talkin' proper agin!" Mom would usually say, "Now, Bonnie, quit tryin' to be so fancy."

After my first year in school, I had learned many new words by learning to read and listening to my teacher. I sometimes, yes often, used them to annoy my brother. Sometimes he seemed to realize and accept that I would continue doing it.

One day that summer, when I was six years old, I had

finished drying the breakfast dishes for Mom, and she said I could go outside and play. Bob was hoeing in the garden on the ridge above the house; I went there.

I asked him, "What are you hoeing?"

"Sweet 'taters," he answered.

I told him, "You're supposed to say sweet potatoes."

He yelled at me, "Git back to the house!" When I didn't leave, he picked up a clod of dirt and threw at the ground by me, not meaning to hit me, but throwing dust on my bare feet. That made me mad! I leaned forward, clenched my fists, and said, "You son of a bitch!"

Bob glanced at me and threw the hoe down, grabbed me by my upper arm with one hand and my wrist with the other, and pulled me toward the house. He yelled at me, "Yer gonna git a whoopin'!"

He scared me, and I said, "Why are you so mad? Was I talking proper again?"

"I'm tellin' Mom! Yer gonna git a whoopin'!" he said, walking fast.

When we got inside the kitchen where Mom was working, Bob told her what I said. She looked startled and surprised, looking straight at me. "Where did you hear those words?" I told her the neighbor boys sometimes said them on the way home from school when they were mad and fighting each other.

She said, "Those are not nice words! Don't ever say them again." She didn't say whether the words were proper, but I never repeated them. She told my brother to stop holding my arm, and when I told her that he had thrown a dirt clod at me, she scolded him.

She forbid my brothers to use bad language around me,

so he seemed disappointed that Mom wasn't mad at me, and I didn't "get a whoopin'" like he would have if he had said the same words.

DADDY ON THE FARM

Daddy was and is my first hero.

Herbert Lewis Lacey—aka "Daddy"—was a smart, hard-working man. He took good care of his family, making sure we were safe, clothed, fed, educated, and enjoyed doing it. He was a learned, self-taught man and smart in business. Members of the community respected, trusted, and depended on him. They looked to him for everything, from politics to veterinary medicine.

Before we moved to our new farm, Daddy and my older brothers had started building the new house. He had carpentry skills and was teaching my brothers. We moved to the farm in the spring even though the house was partially finished. He and the boys wanted to be on the new farm to plow for the spring crops.

My big brothers made split-rail fences from trees on the farm around the barn lot and some of the fields. They put in wire fences where it was difficult to install split-rail fences. Daddy and the boys fenced in the garden with lateral slab strips, cut from the sides of logs used to build the house. The fence kept the rabbits and chickens out of the large enclosed garden. He could get the team of horses with the plow or harrow, inside the fence to plow and smooth the soil. Some of the boys planted the fields, and others worked with Daddy to plant the garden.

When I was five years old, I heard Daddy and the boys talking about planting our spring garden. One morning I looked out the kitchen door and saw them working in the garden. I ran across the road where they were. There were lots of rows marked off for them to plant.

I asked Daddy if I could help. He looked at me and smiled but didn't answer. When I asked again, he said, "Do you really want to help? OK, here's what you can do." He handed me a brown paper bag of seeds, about a pound, and said, "These are radish seeds. Take this row and plant each seed about this far apart." He measured off about an inch with his forefinger and thumb.

I was so excited! I took the seeds' bag, got down on my knees, and planted the whole row, which was over one-hundred feet long. I put a seed about every inch as he told me to do. I covered them and took the few seeds left to Daddy and told him what I did. Of course, he was watching me all the time. He smiled and said, "That's good!" He kept me busy most of the morning, but I'm not sure he thought it would work so well.

Daddy had me watch for the plants to peek up through the ground, keep the weeds pulled and watch for the radishes to grow big enough to eat. I pulled the bigger ones first, then trimmed and washed them for dinner, our noon meal. The radishes lasted several weeks with my careful harvest and handling. I felt so important.

We depended on our horses for transportation, farm work, and our source of power. Daddy could shoe horses, an essential skill in the rocky soil. With no veterinarian close by, and he couldn't have afforded one anyway, he functioned as his own. He could and would stitch up cuts and treat wounds to keep all his animals well.

He had a tall, lean, and nearly white stallion, a half-breed Carriage Horse named Patches. The team's other horse was a large, stocky bay gelding and was a half-breed Percheron named Prince. The two horses seemed like an unlikely match, but Daddy trained them to work well together, especially when they were plowing or pulling heavy loads. He had learned how to manage and train horses when he was a teenager and taught my brothers the same skills.

Daddy acquired a young mare to breed with the stallion. The boys named her Ruby. From the mare and stallion, they raised five foals intending to sell them, I think. But we became attached to them and ended up keeping them all. As they grew, though, they became useful for working on the farm.

Like all our animals, the horses were named and became part of our family. The boys spent many fun hours riding them bareback and without a bridle, out in the fields and pastures. They rode them to the country store and even to town, with bridle and saddle, to pick up groceries.

Tragically, one morning Ruby was found lying down in the water in the creek and couldn't get up. They could not save her and had to "put her down." When my brothers came to the house, all four of them were sobbing. When we younger ones heard the bad news, we all started crying, too. I heard later that the boys had a burial service for Ruby and placed a marker on her grave.

Our Jersey cows were a major source of food and income because their milk contained more cream than other breeds. Mom poured the fresh milk into large crocks. When the cream rose to the top, she skimmed it off and kept it in a cream can. She saved enough cream to churn our butter, which we used sparingly, usually only for breakfast. When the cream can was full, Daddy or one of the boys took it to the country store to sell. The cream brought a good price, enough money to buy supplies Mom needed in the kitchen, and to buy enough bulk peanut butter to fill the cream can over half full, several pounds.

As with our horses, the boys became attached to our cows, and maybe Daddy did. We usually had eight or ten milk cows. We named them all, just like we named our horses. The boys had their favorites and usually claimed one or two as their own, especially after they started milking them, which they did by the time they were twelve years old.

We sorted the calves born in the spring, and the best females were kept for milking and trading or selling for "milkers." The castrated males were shipped to market in the fall for needed money to buy shoes, long underwear, shirts, and winter coats for the boys.

Baby pigs are about the cutest animal, so I think, but when they grow up, not so much! Other important animals on the farm were our hogs. Daddy had a large male hog that the boys named Chief, so they called him "Ol' Chief." Men called him a boar, but women were supposed to say, sire or male hog. Our hog breed was larger than the average full-grown hog and much desired for breeding because it was lean rather than fat like most hogs' breeds.

The sire was the only one of its kind in the community. I

recall men bringing one or more sows past our house hauled in trailers to the barn. They brought their sows to breed with Daddy's choice hog. He made some much-needed money from Ol' Chief's breeding fees.

My brothers liked to ride hogs when they got a chance when Daddy wasn't watching, especially Ol' Chief. A couple of boys would crowd a big hog close to the split-rail fence around the barnyard, and another brother would jump on the hog's back from the fence and see how long he could ride without falling off. Then another brother repeated the game.

The boys always named the sows. They decided to name them after Daddy's several sisters: Pearl, Mary, Laura, and so on. We were taught, though, not to call an adult by just their first name. To be polite, we called the sows Aunt Pearl, Aunt Mary, Aunt Laura, etc. This naming didn't sit well with one aunt when she visited the farm. The other aunts seemed to see the humor in the names.

It is common for male hogs to get mean when they get old. When Ol' Chief became old, it was hard for Daddy and the boys to handle and keep him fenced in. One winter morning, they discovered that the old hog was not in sight. They searched everywhere on the farm but didn't find him. A neighbor came and told Daddy the sire was out on the main gravel road, holding up traffic. He stood in front of a school bus and wouldn't let it pass. The driver tried to chase him away, but Ol' Chief chased him back into the bus and didn't move for over an hour.

The boys and Daddy managed to get Chief back to the barn. They decided they would have to put him down and butcher him. A sad situation, but common on a farm.

Daddy had other good sires to take Ol' Chief's place. It took days to hand-grind the meat, season it for sausage, fry it and pack it in five-gallon crocks to keep it. It was wintertime, or the meat would have spoiled. Over five-hundred pounds of meat became sausage. He made a lot of "good eatin'" that winter.

Daddy didn't usually butcher our hogs because they were needed to send to market in the fall to buy needed feed for the animals. Mom could buy staples, grains, and beans, so she could cook the foods she wanted. There was also a need for soaps, medicines, and other incidentals. And Mom and I could buy our long winter stockings and long underwear for the winter.

Our root cellar was necessary for growing the variety and type of plants wanted. Even if the plants were available elsewhere, the amounts and varieties Daddy wanted would be too expensive. He would have had to pay more because of paying for someone else's labor.

The boys and Daddy dug a root cellar the first summer we were on the new farm. They dug a big cave in the side of the hill below the house. It was an irregular, round shape, about twelve feet in diameter. Because it was underground and had a door, it stayed above freezing in the wintertime, so the seeds and roots for plants would sprout.

They built large wooden boxes on legs, filled with dirt. In late winter, they buried sweet potatoes in the dirt so they could grow "starts." The plants were set outside after the last frost. They raised enough sweet potatoes from the plants, so we had all we wanted to eat. Most importantly, there were many bushels of potatoes to store in the cellar in the fall for the following winter.

Daddy started tomato, sweet and hot peppers, cabbage, and many other seeds that grew into plants to set outside in the spring. The tomatoes and cabbage were a large part of our meals throughout the year. The red and green sweet peppers were eaten raw, and in Mom's cooking, along with the many other vegetables we grew.

The little red-hot peppers got cut up in bean soup, potato soup, and vegetable soup. We kids were eating hot peppers in soups before we could remember. The boys had a way of making a game out of many things. They picked a lot of hot peppers and would see who could eat the most fresh hot peppers. I didn't join in on that game.

Daddy grew crops from seed planted directly in the fields. He grew. more varieties of crops than our neighbors. For the animals, he grew oats and corn. The animals also grazed in the meadows and pastures. He grew a big crop of sugar cane to make sorghum molasses. He fed the leftover sweet fodder after making sorghum molasses to the cows.

For the family's food, there were several crops. The first year on our new farm, Daddy and the boys planted a row of gooseberry plants along the garden's front side. They planted an asparagus bed along the end of the garden. It was about eight feet wide and eighty feet long.

I cut dishpans full of asparagus, about every other day for several weeks in the spring. Mom cooked it for our noon meal. Asparagus, sourdough bread and milk to drink, and maybe a gooseberry cobbler, made a good meal. My first choice!

The red-skinned potatoes were one of Daddy's

biggest crops because they kept well in storage for the winter. They developed fast. Early in the spring some small potatoes, about an inch in size, were dug with our fingers and hands out of the potatoes, and Mom cooked and creamed them with new peas. We had potatoes all summer, fall, and winter. There were always enough potatoes to store for the winter. Potato soup was a regular evening meal, almost always with hot peppers. Mashed or fried potatoes were a standard for the noon meal.

Other crops were Black Diamond watermelons by the hundreds for us to eat and Daddy to sell. There were muskmelons, all we could eat throughout the late summer and fall. Pumpkins were also a big crop. They kept well into the winter. Mom made many pumpkin pies. That was about the only time she made pies. She usually made the berries into cobblers.

Daddy raised bushels of popcorn. It was a fun crop, and we worked together in the fall to hand shell and store it in sealed gallon buckets. There was usually enough popcorn for family and friends to have throughout the winter. In the evenings, we would have fun popping it in our big cast-iron skillet, and each of us had all the popcorn we wanted. Daddy and Mom encouraged us to make fun with whatever we had.

Yet another valuable food for us was honey from bees. Daddy was the "Bee Man" in the community, and he had several bee-hives. Neighbors called on him to cut down hollow trees on their farm where bees had settled in and became a nuisance. He would collect it for half the honey. Sometimes his half would be as much as two washtubs of honey in comb.

The boys and I liked to chew a honeycomb piece with the honey still in it and then chew the comb like chewing gum. We always had many gallons of honey on hand from our hives and the neighbors' trees. We ate honey mixed with peanut butter, on biscuits, sourdough bread, and cornbread. Most of the time, our school lunches were peanut butter and honey sandwiches.

Making sorghum molasses was a challenging but rewarding undertaking. The first year on the farm, Daddy traded and bargained for the parts, then did what it took to put a working sorghum mill together. His sorghum mill was the only one for miles around. A team of horses powered the rollers that squeezed the juice from the sugar cane into heated vats Daddy made. They cooked it until it became thick, making sorghum. It was cooled just enough to pour into gallon buckets. One "cook-off" made several dozen gallons of sorghum and took several hours of the day, with Daddy and the boys working together.

The sorghum was a good source of income for the family because Daddy knew how to cook it. It was labor-intense, but Daddy and the boys seemed to make a game of it. They grew the sugar cane, so there was very little cost there, only labor. He bought hundreds of new, empty gallon buckets in town at a small cost.

They had several cook-offs during late summer, so they made hundreds of gallons of sorghum. He also took buckets of sorghum by wagon into town to sell. I don't know what he charged for the sorghum, but he sold all he wanted to sell. People willingly paid a good price for it.

We kept enough sorghum, so we had all we wanted until the next time to make sorghum rolled around. One year we decided to store our sorghum under a bed. Daddy asked me to count the buckets. The boys carried them to me, and I slid them under the bed in rows. When done, I counted and stored ninety-nine gallons of sorghum under the bed. It sounds like a lot, but for our ten or twelve family members at home, we usually used most of it. Mom used it in baking, and we used it in cooked cereal and on biscuits and sourdough bread for dessert.

The first summer on our farm, Daddy bargained and traded for a used hay baler. A team of horses powered it. To get the hay he neede to feed the livestock through the winter, Daddy and his ready-made work crew baled tons of hay for other farmers for a share of it.

When the location was far away, they would be gone for a few days at a time. They could do that because some of the boys would stay at home to do the chores. They took their food with them. They had a kerosene oil burner to cook beans and cereal, and Mom sent cornbread and sourdough bread with them. They also took watermelons, muskmelons, and tomatoes to round out their meals.

I liked it when Daddy was at home. I would set the table for dinner or supper, then run outside to watch for him to come to the house. When I saw him coming down the barn path, I ran to him and put my small hand in his rough, calloused hand. He would smile down at me. Skipping along to keep up with him, we walked together to the house. This pleasant memory is one of my favorites.

It seemed there was no end to what Daddy could do. In addition to all his outdoor skills, he had learned other skills that he used to benefit the family. One skill was a shoe cobbler. He had acquired the necessary equipment to repair his shoes and the many pairs of my brothers' shoes. The soles of their shoes were worn through but could be removed and replaced. He bought large, flat sheets of leather to make new soles. He traced the shoe's shape needing repair, cut out new soles, removed the old, and tacked on new ones.

He spent many hours in the evening repairing shoes. When someone outgrew their shoes, they were passed down to the next younger brother until the tops wore out, and they had to be discarded. Repairing the boys' shoes was a tremendous saving over buying new shoes or having them repaired. The only cost was the leather and his time. He kept his one pair of work shoes resoled until they were no longer usable, before buying new ones.

Mom's shoes and my shoes were usually given to us by friends and relatives and were not the style that could be repaired. The shoes we received often didn't fit, sometimes too big or too little. If they were pretty dress shoes, I would wear them anyway.

Daddy was an excellent barber. In the fall, just before school started, he cut my brothers' hair. The boys rarely had a bath or washed their hair all summer. They relied on a bar of soap they shared at the swimmin' hole. After the haircut, Mom would wash their hair with a P&G Soap bar and scrub their necks and ears vigorously to be clean for school.

Because there were several brothers, the hair-cutting and scrubbing sessions usually took two or three evenings. The other time they got haircuts was in the spring, which was the norm in the neighborhood. The scrubbing and hair washing were not necessary then because they took baths in our washtub throughout the winter months. And they could go swimmin' again.

Daddy often spent long evenings, especially in the wintertime, sitting at his secretary's desk reading his Bible by lamplight. When I asked him to read the Bible to me, he would have me sit in a chair beside him. He had a pleasant voice as he read the beautiful words of Jesus. That helped me know about God and Jesus at that age.

I watched Daddy one evening, keeping records of the farming expenses and income. He showed me his ledger, where he recorded all the income and expenses, even if it was only a few cents. He said it was important to keep records on the farm because it was a business.

Daddy took his farming seriously. He subscribed to farming journals and journals on the care and breeding of animals. He learned current practices for breeding and managing animals. And he learned to rotate crops to improve crop production on our farm.

He subscribed to the *Weekly Kansas City Star* that came by mail. Through it, he kept up with the stock market to know the best time to ship cattle and hogs in the fall to get the best prices.

We lived in the backwoods on the farm; it wasn't easy to keep up on current events, especially politics. We didn't have a radio, but Daddy heard the news on the radio at the country store and when he went to town, which wasn't often.

Just as important to Daddy, while living on the farm, was reading the day's politics in the *Weekly Kansas City Star*. Even though the news was days old when he got it, he read the details. He was a staunch supporter of Roosevelt, unlike most community residents, and didn't mind getting into one-on-one debates with local men. Because he read so much more and was generally better informed than most of them, he believed he usually won the debates. I heard that the debates generally stayed friendly, but sometimes not.

Local and area news came from the El Dorado Springs weekly newspaper that came in the mail. Daddy liked to keep informed about public issues and never missed a chance to vote. He and Mom voted in all elections.

Daddy believed strongly in free public schools and the opportunity to get a good education. He saw public schools developing and growing in numbers and influence throughout his lifetime and had, himself, taught one-room country schools as a young man. He was, however, self-educated far beyond his teaching education. He strongly supported our local school and was on the school board most of our time on the farm. And due to his carpentry knowledge, he and the neighbors provided some volunteer repair to our schoolhouse.

He didn't spend all his time in the evening at his desk. Often in winter evenings we saw the special fun side come out in Daddy He liked to dance and sing, even though he didn't carry a tune very well, but that didn't stop him. We didn't have a radio or record player, so we made our own music by singing old mountain songs, hoe-downs, waltzes, and two-steps with us kids' and Mom's help.

Daddy taught us to clog dance and jig dance. He and Mom taught us to waltz and square dance. He knew square dance calls and taught the older boys how to call them. Altogether we made a square dance group. We spent many winter evenings entertaining ourselves singing and dancing.

Some evenings were set aside for my brothers and me to read and do our homework. Before I could read, I would ask Daddy to read short stories to me. One of my favorite stories was in Mom's monthly *Lady's Home Journal*. It was "Little Brown Cocoa," a short story about a little negro boy with colorful sketches of him playing with friends. I liked the way they looked.

My brothers couldn't teach me to read. My teacher was frustrated with me and didn't seem to know what to do. One evening I asked Daddy to help me read. He sat me across his knees with the lamplight over my shoulder and had me start reading.

Some words I knew, but when I came to a word I didn't know, he told me, "Just say the word, 'something' and go on reading." After reading a few more words, I usually realized what the word "something" was.

He spent many long evenings, patiently helping me learn

to read. I believe that I became a good reader because of the way he helped me. I realized many years later that I am Dyslexic. Somehow, he managed to help me anyway.

Daddy never talked "baby talk" to me. He always spoke to me and treated me like a grownup. One evening, when I was about eight years old, he and I were talking. I don't remember what we were talking about, but I clearly remember him saying, "Don't let being a girl keep you from doing what you want to do," then we continued with our conversation. I have never forgotten his words that took only a few seconds to say.

In the Fall of 1940, the war threat was in the air, written about in the *Weekly Kansas City Star*. Neighbors were talking among themselves. Workers were needed throughout the country to build new military bases, ammunition plants, and defense plants.

Daddy decided to work as a carpenter to help build the military training base at Fort Leonard Wood, Missouri. There were enough big brothers at home to manage the farm for a while. When he could afford to buy a used car, he was home most weekends.

When work ended at Fort Leonard Wood, he went to Joplin, Missouri, to work on a base they were building there. It was so far away that he seldom came home to the farm. Having the extra money to buy the things we needed and some things we wanted for the first time in my life was nice. But not having Daddy at home all the time was not.

By early fall of '41, Daddy and Mom decided to hold an auction to sell the farm equipment and livestock. The land went back to the previous owner. After the auction, we moved to Joplin in late November. It was good to be able to see Daddy more often. I'm glad we were there when they bombed Pearl Harbor, and the war was declared just a few weeks after we moved.

Our house on the farm was not much more than a shack after it weathered and seasoned. One of Daddy's great regrets was not having resources to build the better house he had planned, due to the Depression. But he taught us always to be thankful for what you have. The lessons we learned on the farm and the love shown there have stayed with me and taught me to live life to the fullest no matter the circumstance, and I believe I have.

Herb Lacey - wagon team on right side

MY FIRST SCHOOL

From the time I can remember, I wanted to go to school with my big brothers. Even though there was no kindergarten in the little country school at that time in Cedar County, Missouri, I started school in the fall of 1936, when I was barely five years old. There were still three more little brothers at home. Mom had also started my two older brothers a year early, a common practice in those hills at that time.

The year I started, a new County Superintendent decreed that a student had to be six years old before January 15th of the next year. My birthday is on March 2nd. I didn't have to leave, but I had to repeat the first grade the following year. I was so upset and mad because 'I knew I was smarter than the other first grader.' Anyway, I thought so!

My brothers taught me how to write my ABCs, say them, and write my name, no printing, only cursive. They taught me to count and write my numbers to 100. I wanted to be able to count money: Pennies, nickels, dimes, and quarters. I thought, "Someday, when I am bigger, I will make money by making dresses for other people like Mom's friend." No one eve told me that women could make money any other way.

Mom made me a new, brightly colored print dress on her treadle sewing machine for the first day of school. I thought it was so pretty. I saw her working on it late at night by the coal oil lamp. The boys had new overalls and a new chambray shirt.

My four brothers and I each got one new pencil

and tablet, and I got a box of Crayolas. I had never seen Crayolas before. It was such a small box, just five colors. Mom said she wished it could be bigger, but they were new, and I was happy to get them. My brothers didn't get any colors. Many of the kids at school didn't get colors; only a tablet and pencil. Because I was the first girl, I got a of colors.

It was about a mile from our house to the one-room country school. My big brother Francis, in the seventh grade, started out holding my hand and walking with me. The other brothers had already run ahead. We were not moving along very fast because my legs were so short. Before I knew what was happening, he picked me up, put me on his back, and put my bare feet in his overalls' hip pockets. We went down the hill on the single wagon-trail, across the bridge, and up the next hill. It was a quarter mile to the main road. With him still carrying me on his back, he ran down the sandy road to the schoolhouse.

As we got close to the schoolhouse, I saw the teacher's new car. It was all shiny and black; it was so pretty. I had never seen anything like it. I had only seen a few old cars and an old truck.

There were many other things I had not seen or heard of before. I could hardly believe the really fancy piano that sounded so pretty. I wanted to learn to play it someday. Also, one big girl whose parents owned a store had a bicycle. I had not heard of a bicycle. I couldn't understand how she could keep it from falling over.

The same girl brought Jell-O in her lunch. It was red, and she showed us how it "shivered." I wondered how it tasted. The teacher brought sandwiches made with "store-bought" bread. I didn't know you could buy bread; Mom made our sourdough bread. Our family's school lunches were usually made of peanut butter and honey sandwiches packed in gallon buckets.

At first, in the classroom, I clung to my big brother. The teacher noticed that I was shy and afraid to speak. There were about fifteen boys and girls in school, and some boys were as big as men. The teacher allowed me to sit with my seventh-grade brother, across the classroom in a double desk. I was not close to the only other first-grader. After a few weeks, I had to sit with her at a double desk. I was gradually becoming less shy.

I idolized my first teacher. My first year at school was the teacher's first year at the same school. She brought a set of World Books and a world globe to school that fall. She probably bought them with her own money. She also checked out books, especially for older students, from the library in town because our school library was small and limited. My brothers and other students checked out books for themselves and our parents to read.

I was surprised to learn that the world was round and turned from the globe she brought. I was afraid I could fall off the earth, but the teacher said, "No, gravity holds us from falling." I didn't know what gravity was, but I trusted her. I looked at the World Books almost every day, even before I could read, and asked the teacher many questions. I was no longer shy.

I was, and always will be, left-handed. There were no other left-handed students in the school. The teacher and my family were constantly hassling me about using my left hand. They said I would be "handicapped" for life. At that age, I didn't know what handicapped was, but it sounded scary. Could I be crippled? The teacher did not punish me, but she watched me. When she saw me holding the pencil with my left hand, she would walk by and take the pencil from my hand, put it in my right hand, and tell me, firmly, "Use your right hand." I gradually changed over to writing with my right hand. They hassled me about throwing with my left hand, but I refused to change to my right hand to throw a ball.

The country school had a wood-burning stove for heat when the weather was cold and windows to open when the weather was hot. We had two outhouses, one for boys and one for girls; some schools did not. Our drinking water was carried in from the well in a bucket. For the first time in that school, the teacher had us all bring our own tin drinking cups, rather than all the students sharing the same dipper.

Since there was no church in the community, the school was the gathering place for activities. One entertainment in the school community was "Literaries" at night, one in the fall and one in the spring. Anyone who wanted to play an instrument, sing a song, dance, recite a poem, or entertain could do so. My brothers and I usually did something, as did most of the students and also some parents. Coal oil lamps for the night programs were the only light, so one of my brothers went in early to light them. One of my brothers went in early to start a fire in the wood-burning, heating stove in cold weather.

Another popular program was "Box Suppers." Teenage

girls and young single women decorated a big box and packed it with sandwiches and a piece of pie or cake, enough for a meal for two. Those of us younger girls who wanted to make boxes and pack them with special goodies were not allowed to because the teenage boys and young men buying the boxes, would not have liked it. They did not want a box that belonged to a little girl.

The box owner was supposed to be a secret, but word sometimes got out as to who owned them. A certain boy usually wanted to buy a certain girl's box, and if they were sure which one it was, they would pay more to get it. They auctioned off the boxes to the highest bidder. The highest price was usually about twenty-five cents; most of the time, less. The money from the sales went to buy school supplies.

But, the most popular of all happenings was the Christmas Program held at Christmastime at night. At that time, most homes did not have a Christmas tree. Only schools and churches had Christmas trees. The teacher always had a beautiful Cedar tree that the older students cut from a farmer's pasture, with his permission. All the students, big and small, made decorations. There were popcorn ropes, stars cut from colored paper, and snowflakes cut of white paper. The teacher furnished all the "store-bought" decorations. The tree was so pretty and smelled so good.

All the kids participated in the program, either by singing solos, singing in groups, or reciting poems. No one was left out. The students drew names for a gift exchange, with the gifts costing ten cents or less. Then the teacher provided treats for all the students and their families.

I attended the school for over five years with the same

teacher. She never physically punished a student. We all knew that if a student misbehaved, our parents would be told, and handle the necessary discipline. Seldom did anyone misbehave.

One of the first things I remember about the teacher was she didn't allow anyone to say, "I can't." She would have us say, "I'll try," then she and other students would work with the child to learn the task. Learning never to say, "I can't," but to say, "I'll try" and do it and succeed were important and defining lessons.

Bonnie's Second Grade Class
(Bonnie – second from bottom right)

SO MANY FIRSTS AT CHRISTMASTIME

Being born in a back-woods community in rural Missouri, we were very isolated. At five years of age, in 1936, I had never been to town. One reason was we didn't have a car, only a team of horses and a wagon. Only rarely did any family have a car, and the town was about ten miles away.

I went to our one-room country school with my five older brothers. As Christmastime drew near, I heard that the small town would give a bag of candy and an orange—I didn't know what an orange was—on Saturday before Christmas to all the grade school students in the district if we came to town. They also said the movie picture showman would give a free ticket to see the movie "Heidi" with Shirley Temple. I had never seen a movie picture.

So, on that Saturday morning before Christmas, Daddy and the boys hurried to do the chores while Mom cooked breakfast and made a big box of peanut butter sandwiches for lunch. Mom said the food in town costs too much. I had heard before that when something cost too much, I couldn't have it.

We ate an early breakfast, then Daddy and the boys harnessed the horses' team up to the wagon. Our family of nine kids and Mom and Daddy climbed into the wagon. It was cold, so we sat in the wagon bed on heavy quilts and covered with more quilts, wearing heaving coats, stocking caps, and billed hats for the older boys. Mom and Daddy climbed up on the spring seat in front, with Mom holding my baby brother, a toddler, wrapped up in warm blankets.

Even though it was cold, we were too excited to care about a snow blanket on the ground. The horses also were spirited and ready to go. We drove down the hill, across the homemade wooden bridge, and up the next steep hill to the main road, about a quarter mile from our house. We turned onto the gravel road and headed to town.

The cedar trees had snow piled high. It was so pretty. Then, after about an hour, Daddy turned onto the highway that ran by the town. The road looked so different. The boys said it was concrete; I had never seen concrete.

Daddy then turned onto the street to go downtown, and we ran over some big, shiny rods lying across the street. I was scared because they were so bumpy under the metal wagon wheels. The boys said they were supposed to be there; they were train tracks. I had never heard of trains, so I asked, "What are trains?" They said they were big engines that pulled boxcars. I still didn't understand it!

Now we were on a brick street, and shiny cars were passing us. And there were such beautiful houses like I had never seen before. They were brick, stone, and they painted some white, yellow, and blue. They decorated them with bright lights, and wreaths with Santa Clauses and snowmen in the yards.

Then I looked ahead and saw a wonderland of bright, colorful lights and decorations along the streets and storefronts everywhere. Mom said they were 'lectric lights. It was the first time I saw electric lights.

Daddy tied the team up, and we jumped out, smiling and laughing, so excited. We hurried to the Community Building to get in line for our treats. As we waited in line, I could hear music, but I saw no one playing guitars or fiddles or singing. Mom said it was a record. I had never heard of a record.

We got our sack of candy and an orange, and then the whole family walked on the sidewalks. The boys said the walks were concrete. I had never seen sidewalks before.

Soon we saw Santa coming toward us. I think he noticed our large family. Daddy was carrying my three-year-old brother. Since Santa was eye-to-eye with him, he paid special attention to my little brother, talking and laughing with him. When Santa walked on, my little brother said, "Daddy, 'dats not whiskers, 'dats jes' totten on his face!" Beards were common in the rural community, and he knew the difference between cotton and real hair.

We all headed for the Ben Franklin Store, or as some called it, "The Five and Dime Store." As we stepped inside, I couldn't believe my eyes: It seemed there were electric lights, garlands, ornaments, silver icicles, and angels everywhere. I had heard of angels; now I knew how they looked.

The boys headed for boy's toys, and Mom and I headed for girl's toys. There were teddy bears, play dishes, doll furniture, and dolls. I headed for the baby dolls piled on a big tabletop. Some were big, and some were small. I picked up several and held them in my arms to check how they fit. Then I saw one tiny doll in just a diaper. I picked her up and held her, just the right fit and softness. Her skin was brown. I had never seen a brown doll before. Mom said it was a Negro doll and that some people have brown skin. I didn't know that!

I looked at the tag, and it read 59 cents. I asked Mom if I could have it. She said we would have to ask Daddy. He came over and looked at the tag. He said it cost too much. I knew not to make a fuss if he said it cost too much, so I laid it back down.

We went out to the wagon and stood around, eating our sandwiches. We went to the natural spring and drank water from a tin cup Mom brought for us.

Then Mom said it was one o'clock, time to go to the picture show. Daddy said to hurry back after the picture show, so we could get home to do the chores.

The movie house was crowded and noisy with all the school kids. As I tried to watch and hear, I couldn't understand how I could see the people in the picture, and they were not there. And it upset me that the woman who was so mean to Heidi.

When the movie was over, we hurried to the wagon. Daddy had fed the horses at noon, but they were ready to move on. So, we climbed back in the wagon to head for home, so Daddy and the boys could do the chores: feed the horses, cows, pigs, and chickens, and milk the cows. Then Mom would have a good, hot supper ready. By that time, we would be starving after just having sandwiches for lunch.

A few days later, we woke up early on Christmas morning to see what Santa Claus had put in our stockings. I checked my stocking but did not notice what anyone else got, because the Negro baby doll was in my stocking.

An older brother had already told me that Daddy was Santa: That made the doll even more special!

CALL OF NATURE

Outside, the whip-poor-wills are calling me as I dry the dishes. I can't dry the big things, because Mom says I'm too little, just five years old, and the pans are too heavy.

Mom says I can go outside and play now.

The sun is going down behind the garden fence, so I'm going to my favorite evening place. I sit down on the green grass and rest against the picket fence that Daddy and the boys made. I listen to the birds sing and watch the clouds as the sun goes to bed. Daddy says the sun goes to bed just like we do.

It sounds like the soft wind is whispering and singing in the trees. Whip-poor-wills and mockingbirds are singing, flying around, catching bugs, then settling into their nests for the night. Crows are darting 'round and making loud noises. The cows are softly mooing in the pasture while the frogs are croaking, close-by, down by the creek.

The sky is bright blue overhead with lots of fluffy, white clouds floating by and changing shapes. Down low, the sun is making bright colors on the clouds. I have only seen pictures of elephants, polar bears, and angels. As all the birds are singing, I watch the clouds and see white elephants, polar bears, angels and sometimes peoples' faces. But they soon change into something else as they float across the pretty blue sky.

The sun has almost gone to sleep now, and I can hardly see it. A screech owl screeches and one hoot owl hollers, then another, then another. Soon it sounds like they are talking and answering each other.

Mom is calling me. "Bonnie, it's time to come in now!"

Inside the kitchen door, it's kinda dark. Mom says they won't light the coal oil lamps so we can save oil. Besides, everyone is tired. They will get up early in the morning to do the chores and eat breakfast, so Daddy and the boys can work in the fields before it gets so hot. I go to my bed, take off my dress and climb in.

What's that? The ole speckled rooster is crowing outside my window, telling me it's time to wake up. I musta gone to sleep. I open my eyes and see it's getting light outside. Mom is rattling the iron stove lids and putting wood in the cookstove to cook breakfast. I will help her. I'll set the table and help stir the gravy.

Oh, good! I didn't pee the bed like I sometimes do. Now, Mom won't call me a pee-tail, but I better get to the outhouse quick. Pulling my dress on over my slip and bloomers, I hurry to the door, barefoot. My little rooster is crowing outside the door. The chickens are clucking, scolding, and pecking in the grass for bugs. Little birds are singing in the trees, and the sun is shining through the leaves. I know the birds got here from the other side of the house, by flying over, but how did the sun get over here on this side of the house? I must ask Daddy.

Oh! Oh! I better hurry on quickly, or I won't get to the outhouse in time. Sometimes I see the boys pee behind a tree, but Mom said little girls are not supposed to do that. The boys would tell on me if I did. If I don't make it to the outhouse, will Mom call me a pee tail? Maybe I won't tell her if I don't make it in time and pee my bloomers.

Whew! I made it in time! Now I can hurry to the kitchen and help Mom.

CHURCH IN THE SCHOOLHOUSE

There were no churches in our community close enough to get to by team and wagon. One day I heard the neighbors and kids talking about a preacher coming to have a church in the schoolhouse. I wondered what church was, and Mom told me it was about Jesus. I heard her singing about God and Jesus most of the time while working in the kitchen. I loved to hear her sing but didn't understand what it was all about. I was five years old.

It was a beautiful summer Sunday morning when the preacher was coming. Daddy and the boys hurried and fed the animals and milked the cows. They dressed up in their good overalls, chambray shirts, and hand-tied neckties. All the boys and men wore neckties to church. I wore my best dress.

I helped Mom cook her usual big breakfast. After we all ate, Daddy and the boys hooked up the team to the wagon, and my brothers and I climbed in. Daddy sat on the spring seat in front., and then we headed for the schoolhouse over a mile away. Mom stayed home with our youngest brother.

As we got close, I heard the piano playing and people singing. I had never heard anything like it. It sounded pretty. Inside, our school friends and neighbors filled the room. Some were standing because the room was so crowded.

When we started singing, I thought one song was the prettiest of all: "Brighten the Corner Where You Are." When I asked Daddy later what the words meant, he said,

"It tells us to be happy and help each other when they have troubles."

I thought, "That's what Daddy and Mom do for our neighbors." They always seemed happy helping others.

The preacher talked about the Golden Rule: "Do to others what you want them to do to you." He talked loudly. Everyone there seemed happy, clapping their hands and hollering, but I was getting tired. Then we sang again for a long time, and I was getting hungry.

When we got home from church, I asked Mom if she knew, "Brighten the Corner Where You Are." She sang the whole song from memory, and I soon learned most of it, even though I didn't understand most of the words.

I didn't know at the time that I wouldn't get another chance to go to church for three more years. They never had church in the schoolhouse again while we were living there. The songs, the preacher's words, and hearing the Golden Rule, which is Jesus' words, made a lasting impact on my life. Mom and Daddy set the example of caring and how to treat others, even my brothers...

That was the hardest!

LIZZIE HICKS

Lizzie Hicks was well known, respected, and admired in our rural neighborhood. Her husband owned the country store with a gas station next to their farm. It seems he spent most of his time with his customers, who were neighbors. So, she did most of the work on their small farm.

Adult women were usually called Miss or Mrs., by us kids. I only spoke of her, though, using the full name of Lizzie Hicks.

I was five years old the first time I saw her. I remember her wearing a long calico dress with long sleeves and men's shoes. She had never been cut her long hair and she had it tucked in a bun under her sunbonnet. She was walking behind a plow, cultivating her garden. Someone told me she also plowed and cultivated fields with a team of horses.

They had built their unique house into the side of a hill. The back wall and side walls were the stone that was naturally there. The front of the upstairs opened at ground level on the other side of the house.

I came to know Lizzie Hicks when her teenage daughter, Alean, showed me their house. Alean later married my brother, Lonnie. She showed me the house's upstairs rooms, furnished with ornate, Victorian furniture from better days.

The family lived in the lower level of the house, furnished with primitive, functional furniture where Lizzie Hicks did her cooking. She was well known for her wonderful cooking, especially at church dinners. Some of her other tasks were canning, washing on the washboard, sewing on her treadle sewing machine, to name a few. That was after she finished working in the fields and garden.

When the community built their first church, Lizzie Hicks attended most of the services any time the doors were open. She had a couple of nice dresses and a nice sunbonnet or hat. Women were expected to wear a head covering in church. I saw her there once in her "church clothes." She was an attractive woman as she smiled and sang enthusiastically.

As I grew up, Alean became my sister-in-law, and we became good friends. One day we talked about her mother and how strong she was in both body and character.

Smiling, Alean said, "Did you ever hear the story about Mom getting mad at a rich neighbor man?" I answered, "No," so she told me this true story....

One day my friend and I were walking home from our country grade school. It had snowed all day and was about a foot deep. We were walking in the tracks in the middle of the dirt road.

My friend and I looked up and saw our "rich neighbor" coming down the middle of the road in his new car. He didn't slow down. We jumped into the ditch with the snow up to our waists, to keep from being run over. He just drove on.

When I got home, I was covered with wet snow, and I was freezing cold. Mom and Dad were both at home. When Mom saw me, she asked, "What happened?" When I told her, she told Dad to harness up the horse and wagon.

He said, "No, not while you are so mad!"

She harnessed them herself. "Get the ball bat."

"No, not while you are so mad!" he repeated.

"I am not going to allow my daughter to be disrespected by that rich man."

She got the bat, climbed into the wagon, and took off down the road. It was nighttime, but there was moonlight. She drove to the neighbor's house.

When she knocked on the door the man's wife came to the door. Her husband had gone to bed. When Mom told her happened, she said, "Give me that bat."

Outside the door my mom, could hear the man hollering and screaming as his wife beat him with the bat.

Alean said her mom heard how the man was bruised and injured and could not get out of bed for a couple of days. She said the story is true and is a legend in the community.

Everyone knew Lizzie Hicks for her strength, character, and justice. She lived up to it!

OH! MY TOE!

There was an old log lying in the backyard. The bark had fallen off, so it was smooth. It was several feet long and really big around. I was six years old, and my little brothers and I liked to climb on it and run across it, trying not to fall off. The older brothers used it for a chopping block to split the wood for Mom's cookstove.

Late one afternoon, I saw my ten-year-old brother, James, chopping wood. I climbed up on the log and stood there, barefoot, watching him.

He yelled at me, "Git back in the house!"

I yelled back, "No, I don't have to!"

As I stood there, James continued chopping wood. Then, acting like the ax slipped, he chopped into the log, close to my feet, trying to scare me. It didn't work.

Trying again, he reached out toward my feet with the ax.

The ax stuck into the log. But it cut the end of my big toe at the back of my toenail, cutting through the bone.

I jerked my foot away. The end of my toe dropped over, hanging by a thin strip of skin and was bleeding.

I sat down on the log and started screaming at the top of my lungs. Daddy and two older brothers, who were plowing in the fields, heard the screaming and came running to see what was wrong.

When Daddy saw my toe, he pressed the end back in place and sent one of the boys to ask our neighbor who had a pickup, to come over and take us to town to the doctor.

Daddy carried me inside to the kitchen, and Mom wiped the blood until my toe stopped bleeding.

Mom and Daddy relied a lot on folk medicine at that time. The tradition was that Native Americans used tobacco as a pain reliever and healing medicine. Daddy just happened to have a chew of his home-grown tobacco in his mouth. He carefully pressed the tobacco on my toe and Mom wrapped it. Those were the days before antibiotics.

Our neighbor drove up in his pickup and took Daddy and me to town about ten miles away. The neighbor had called the doctor who was waiting in his office when we arrived. Daddy carried me in and sat me on the exam table. As the doctor unwrapped my toe, I could tell he was angry when he saw the tobacco there. I heard him quietly say "filthy," and saying other words I had never heard before.

He laid his instruments and needles and thread on the exam table beside me. Daddy watched as the doctor rinsed my toe carefully and picked the little pieces of tobacco from the wound with small tongs. Pressing the end of my toe back in place, he decided not to do stitches, and then he wrapped my toe in bandages.

The doctor told Daddy to unwrap my toe every morning and soak it in warm Epsom Salts solution for about an hour, then wrap it in clean, dry dressings and not to let my toe get wet, except when soaking it. In a couple of weeks, my toe had healed without being disfigured. And my toenail eventually grew back.

Mom and Daddy were convinced and relied on Epsom Salts for treating wounds after that. And I don't remember Daddy ever again using chewing tobacco on a sore or wound.

THE WIENIE ROAST

The schoolkids are talking about the "Wienie Roast" we will have at school. They will build a big bonfire in the schoolhouse yard and roast wienies and "mushmellas."

I ask my brothers what wienies and mushmellas are. They say, "You'll see!" I know I'm not supposed to ask any more questions. I heard my brothers talking about wienies, laughing, and whispering. I'm not supposed to hear. *What is mushmellas?*

I just started school for the first time. Our new schoolteacher is so nice. She says she will bring wienies and marshmallows for a wienie roast in the schoolhouse yard. She invited all the families of the school kids so we could meet and get acquainted.

The wienie roast is tonight. Daddy and the boys feed the animals, milk the cows, and take the milk to Mom to strain. I can see she isn't cooking supper. I don't understand why. Daddy and the boys hook the horses up to the box wagon. We all jump in and head over the dirt road to the schoolhouse.

Why didn't we eat supper? "What are we going to eat?"

The daddies and the big boys start the bonfire from wood they piled up. They have long sticks in a pile by the fire. The fire is so pretty and warm, and the sunset is beautiful. I don't know what is going on, and I am so hungry. Mom's cornbread and beans would taste good about now.

The teacher has the boys carry big grocery bags full of

food from her car. There are wienies, buns, and mushmellas. The kids say it is what we will eat, "wienies and mushmellas."

Moms, daddies, and kids put the wienies on the long sticks' end and roasted them over the bonfire. We put them on a bun with mustard and start eating them. They give me one, then two. "So, this is what wienies are!"

We roast wienies until everyone has all they can eat. Some boys and men ate three or four wienies on buns. Then we roast the pretty, fluffy mushmellas. I roast some mushmellas on a stick, and they taste so good. The kids play hide-and-seek. It's starting to get dark. Now it's time to head for home.

The daddies and boys put out the bonfire with water from the well's pump. Some families have cars or teams and wagons, but some have to walk home, a mile or more. Daddy invites our neighbors, who are walking, to ride with us. We all jump into our wagon and head for home.

As we ride along, I'm thinking, "I didn't miss supper after all." Mom's cornbread and beans are good, but the wienies are better.-But I won't tell her that!

"Now I know what wienies are…. I think."

MISS ETSENHAUSER

The first time I saw Miss Etsenhauser, she walked into our new country church one cool, spring evening, just as we were singing our first song. Strangers were uncommon in those backwoods' hills in the mid-thirties. The genteel woman made the surprise appearance, and heads turned to follow her movement.

Her appearance and manner were strikingly different than the local people were accustomed to seeing. She wore a perky velvet French beret pulled down on one side over her silvery-grey Dutch-bobbed hair. Bright blue eyes opened wide beneath cropped bangs. Thin, rounded shoulders betrayed her years, but the firm set of her chin and her head's tilt suggested her defiance of time. Her colorful silk print dress flowed loosely over her diminutive frame down to her ankles where sturdy walking shoes protruded from under the hem.

When we finished the first song, the preacher heartily welcomed our fascinating guest, the first visitor to our congregation of about thirty people. Her exploring eyes needed no spectacles as she seemed to acknowledge everyone and everything in the little church.

Her focus returned to the ornate pump organ which sat idle in front of the room after looking around. No one in the congregation knew how to play it. Noticing her interest in the organ, the preacher asked Miss Etsenhauser if she would like to play for the services.

Smiling and without hesitation, she went straight to the organ and sat down on the blue, plush covered stool. She seemed transcended to another time and place with her feet pumping, elbows akimbo, and hands flying over the keys. We watched with joy and sang with gusto to match the music, the first of many times she played the organ at our church.

Miss Etsenhauser reflected an aura of refinement and culture never before known in our rural community, tempered with an unorthodox flair for humor. The neighbors talked among themselves, wondering from where she came. She was secretive about her past life, but her way of talking so "proper," her knowledge of the world, and her ability to play musical instruments led us to believe she had an education in the "big city."

Miss Etsenhauser seemed to have "come from nowhere." She had recently moved into an abandoned farmhouse about a mile from us. When I heard her playing the organ at church, I told Daddy I wished I could play the organ like Miss Etsenhauser. A few days later, he came home with an old pump organ, like at church. He bought it at an auction. He made arrangements with her to give me lessons in exchange for stove wood he and my brothers cut and hauled to her.

Stepping inside the old ramshackle cottage for my first lesson was like a glimpse into another world for me. She had beautiful, old-world antiques like I had only seen in pictures. I saw some of the things were an ornate settee, handsome side chairs, lavish tables, beveled mirrors, oil paintings and colorful oriental rugs. The room reflected her mysterious past.

One piece of furniture dominated the parlor: the ornate,

handsome, massive, upright piano. All the furniture in the room was arranged around it. It wasn't easy to keep my mind on the lessons, surrounded by the remarkable splendor. Some of the simple melodies I learned on her piano are still with me.

During the summer, I took lessons from her, and she played beautiful classical music for me. But she taught me more than music, carefully avoiding mentioning herself, a lesson in itself. Through the music and the surroundings, she inspired me to become conscious of other people and other lands and cultures.

Never mind Miss Etsenhauser's genteel ways and diminutive size. She seemed to thrive in the hill country, planting gardens and small crops, sometimes with other farmers' help. She hired help when she needed it, seeming not to lack for money. Knowing how to care for animals, she had chickens, pigs, and cows. At first, our neighbors often ridiculed her. They soon accepted her and recognized they would do well to practice some of her methods.

She knew how to care for livestock, and it became known she had "a way with animals." Neighbors sought advice from her about animals' care and asked her to come and "doctor" their sick animals in exchange for something she needed.

Because of her wide range of interests and knowledge, from world affairs to the sheer joy of living, Miss Etsenhauser helped in many ways to make living easier in our neighborhood. She lauded homemaking and living off the land, walking everywhere she went, visiting with neighbors. She easily talked with both women and men about their interests, sometimes advising them without their knowing it. I feel she could have talked equally as well with presidents and kings, maybe she had.

Being a child of eight years, I never completely lost my timidity in the grand and noble woman's presence, so strangely different from me or anyone I knew. For all her unassuming manner and diminutive size, she always seemed larger than life. Her remarkable talents and qualities were astounding to me. For decades in my adult life, I tried to acquire the kinds of antique furniture she had in her parlor.

I can still feel the grief and loss that welled up inside me when I learned Miss Etsenhauser had moved away as silently as she came. Yet so much of her knowledge, warmth, and joy lingered with the isolated hill people and me. It remains with me eight decades later.

LIFE AFTER THE FARM

Leaving the farm was an emotional and life-changing time in my early life. I said goodbye to close neighbors, school friends, my teacher, and close relatives. I entered a world unknown to me.

Daddy was working on a military base near Joplin, Missouri. Just before Thanksgiving, in 1941, we left the farm and moved outside of Joplin, to an old stone farmhouse we rented where we could keep our cow. The house had electricity and pretty papered walls; all of these for the first time in my life.

Mom adapted readily to leaving the farm. Because she had money to buy foods from the store, she had less of a workload. She made her yeast bread only as she wanted to because we could buy "store-bought" bread. She kept her cookstove but didn't like burning coal instead of wood. And she liked our new house because it had pretty papered walls.

But I didn't like the coal we used in our stoves. I thought It was "stinky." We burned hickory, cedar, and other woods in our stoves on the farm. The fragrance of cedar and other woods were in the air. Near Joplin, the air smelled strong and stinky because they mined coal and burned it in area stoves.

We didn't see Daddy often because he was working long hours, sometimes seven days a week. The family was together, though, in the evenings. After supper, we sat around the radio listening to music or comedy programs.

I remember one "as needed" ritual repeated several

times throughout the winter. Daddy would mix a "Hot Toddy." He claimed it was a well-known "remedy" for curing colds. In the wintertime, he kept a bottle of whiskey "for medicinal purposes only." He stirred hot water, honey, and a little whiskey together and mixed it well. As he sat in a chair, my brothers and I filed by, and he gave each of us a large "sip" of the Hot Toddy. I don't know whether it worked or not, but I thought the drink tasted good!

One Sunday morning, the family was listening to church music on our new radio. It was December 7, 1941. An announcer interrupted the program and said they had bombed Pearl Harbor and killed hundreds of sailors and others. Stunned by the news, we all sat down and listened. I thought about my two brothers in the military and three more who were draft age. Roosevelt declared war the next day.

Mom was overwhelmed, knowing she had five sons eligible for the draft, and another soon would be. One son was already in the Navy on the USS Wichita and went into combat at once.

In the following days before Christmas, it seemed all we heard was bad news. Even my rowdy brothers were quiet and sad. Feeling lost and alone in all the trauma, I worried about what was going to happen. I was not sleeping well, and was having bad dreams, even nightmares.

One night I dreamed I was walking to the evening Christmas program at school. We lived on a sideroad back from a busy highway where trucks drove by in the night. There was a nightclub on the other side of the road with lots of cars and loud noise.

I awakened from a dream and found myself on my way to school. It was about a quarter of a mile from our house. Barefoot, wearing a petticoat and bloomers, I walked beside the highway on sharp gravel. Trucks and cars were honking at me. I quickly turned and ran back to our house and crawled into my parents' bed at their feet, cold and shivering. Mom asked, "How did you get so cold?" I didn't answer, afraid I would get into trouble.

The next morning Mom and Daddy noticed that my feet were dirty, bruised, cut, and bleeding from the sharp gravel. They were shocked when I told them what happened, but they believed me. I sleep-walked a few more times, but never went outside again.

Just before my birthday, March 2nd, we again moved to a small farm closer to town. Daddy bought it so we wouldn't have to pay rent. And they wanted to keep the boys out of trouble by keeping them busy. The house needed restoring, but we could plant small fields and make a garden. He helped when he had time. He added cows, pigs, chickens, and a horse, for work, food, and fun. Mom, as always, made the best of it. Daddy thought we would be staying there when the war was over, where his father, a brother and a sister lived.

Mom started driving our car. She had driven a car when she was younger and didn't need a license. Daddy rode to work with others, so Mom had the car all the time.

When we weren't working in the garden or caring for the animals, Mom drove us to town, especially on Saturday. Daddy gave each of us kids a quarter allowance each week. The boys spent their quarters by going to the matinee movies, buying popcorn and pop. I thought all the westerns were the same, so I went to the dime store, discovering new things and looking at prices, seldom buying anything. Mom usually stayed with my little sister and me.

Every day I listened to a singer I liked on the radio. She sang country, western, and folk songs and yodeled with most of them. I memorized her songs but couldn't figure out how to yodel. I heard them talking about a book that teaches how to yodel, for $2.00. Without telling anyone, I decided to save my quarters for the book. I knew I'd need eight.

One day I asked Daddy to change my quarters into dollar bills. He asked me what I was going to do with the money. I told him I would send $2.00 to order a book through the mail to teach me how to yodel. He was quiet for a moment then asked me, "Have you thought about that? Do you think you can learn to yodel from a book?" I then realized that learning to yodel from a book probably wasn't possible. I soon decided how else to spend the money.

I had been looking at things in the dime store that I would like to buy. I noticed that there were girl's panties that I didn't know about before. I had never had anything but bloomers that Mom and I made. I spent the whole $2.00 on panties. No more bloomers, ever. A real breakthrough for me in my life.

During the summer, Mom took us to the library once a week. We wandered through the rows of books, searching for the ones we wanted to read. Mom checked out Harold Bell Wright's books, history books, and novels books for herself and Daddy. We spent time at home reading and playing. The boys and I worked when we needed to or had to.

That fall, Daddy took a carpentry supervisor position near Lawrence, Kansas, to build an ammunition plant, because he felt the job was essential for the war effort. He moved our family to Winchester, Kansas, because housing was scarce and expensive near Lawrence. The rented, two-story, brick house there was the nicest we ever had with electricity, running water, and a bathroom. He would be home only on weekends and often had to work then. I missed seeing him every day again.

But we only enjoyed it for a few months. Since Daddy didn't like to pay rent, he bought an old abandoned ornate and beautiful Victorian house near the town center. The boys and I helped Mom with renovation for months and moved into it in the spring; Daddy was away working in Lawrence. My brothers and I worked with Mom, continuing to paint, paper, and clean. Mom hired paper hangers to paper the two-story curved stairway walls. We had a phone for the first time but had an outhouse. The house became a showpiece in the town and a gathering place for our friends.

Mom liked being close to the two grocery stores in town, and her cooking was changing. She often sent one of us to get groceries she needed or wanted. We bought canned meats, packaged pasta, breakfast cereals, and bread. She bought canned foods for what we couldn't grow in our garden. For the first time in her life, she made her special dishes when and as she wished.

Mom became my Mom like I had never known. There were several widows in Winchester whose husbands left them with a car. They didn't know how to drive and didn't want to learn. As it became known that Mom drove a car, the women hired her to drive them to nearby towns to shop. She shopped in resale shops and bought her and my pretty dresses, coats, and shoes. She also bought new clothes. She altered them when needed but no longer made our dresses.

The town had four churches in town within easy walking distance from our house. I went to church with my girlfriend and occasionally, to Miss Young's church. There was a church across the street from us where I went at times. Going to church was a treat to me, and I went somewhere to church most Sundays.

A deacon could teach Bible Study in the school one hour each week. He had us memorize Bible verses, which I liked doing, and committed many scriptures to memory. And I memorized all the books of the Bible in order, and still remember them.

The town was limited in what it had to offer. The Post Office didn't have home delivery, so we had to go to the post office to get our mail. There were two grocery stores, a service station, a hardware store, and a saloon. We, however, didn't lack for fun. We made our fun by playing sports and other games, kids and adults often playing together. We played outside and used the high school and gym when not in use by the school.

An outside traveling picture show came to town once a week on Saturday night in the summertime. I popped and sold popcorn to earn free admission, and all the popcorn I could eat. My brothers set up chairs on the ground and earned free passes to the movie.

Meanwhile, the war was raging, and Mom had four sons in the thick of battle. By the time we received the few letters, they were many weeks old. The date and location on the letter would be blacked out. Parents would sometimes be notified of their son's death and receive letters from their son many weeks later.

The war was foremost in the minds of us all. First thing in the morning, Mom turned on the radio for the latest news. One of my brothers delivered the daily *Kansas City Star* newspaper for the small town, starting at 4:00 AM. She insisted that he bring her a newspaper first. We did all we could to help her with what she needed and wanted.

The invasion of Normandy in the summer of 1944 brought new fears for all who had soldiers in that area. It was months before Mom knew if her sons survived. The war continued intensely for many months, but the combat came to an end in the summer of 1945. Finally, the tensions, stress, and fatigue of having her sons in combat began to ease. All her sons came home alive.

One of my brothers was slightly injured in Europe after the war was over but fully recovered. Many servicemen were still traumatized from all the years of combat. The condition, now known as PTSD, was called "Shell Shock" or "Battle Fatigue," but was not treated. At fourteen years, I was also concerned for Mom and felt that she could not get past the war's impact on her life. She was doing the necessary tasks to provide for the family, but she was no longer singing or smiling as she did on the farm.

For the first time since leaving the farm and the start of the war, Mom could fully enjoy the advantages she now had to make life easier. Daddy's defense work was over, and he was home all the time. Since he was there for us kids, Mom took a bus trip to Wichita to visit my brother, Don, and his family for several days.

One evening my girlfriend and I decided to walk to "downtown," just a block away in the small town. I had a quarter to buy treats for us. As we got close to the "restaurant/beer joint," we decided to buy a cigarette pack. Some of Daddy's sisters and nieces smoked cigarettes, and I saw movie stars smoking. We wanted to try it. We went inside, and I told the man I wanted to buy a pack of cigarettes for Daddy. Because he knew me and trusted me, he sold me a pack for ten cents.

As we stepped out the door, I saw Daddy coming down the sidewalk and knew he would buy cigarettes. I knew the man would tell Daddy what I had done. I hid the cigarettes so Daddy wouldn't see them as we walked past him, then I gave them to my girlfriend and ran home. We were on daylight-savings-time, so it was not yet dark. No one was home. I dressed in my pajamas, crawled into bed, and waited, and waited.

It had started to get dark when Daddy came into my room and pulled a chair up beside my bed. He didn't say anything for the longest time. Finally, he said, "I just always hoped you wouldn't do that." He looked and sounded so sad. His words pierced my heart, and I stifled a sob. After a while, he left the room.

Nothing else was ever said to me. I'm sure he told Mom when she came home from her trip. I never smoked after hearing what Daddy said. Oh, I've taken puffs on others' cigarettes, but never started smoking, knowing how it would have grieved his heart.

But there was not enough fulltime carpenter work in Winchester for him to earn a living. And we felt isolated, being so far from our extended family in Missouri.

Mom and Daddy decided to move to Rich Hill, Missouri, where Daddy would start a carpentry business, building, remodeling, and restoring houses. And we would be close to our family in Cedar County. Mom and Daddy bought a house at the edge of town, so that we could have our animals and a team of horses. Daddy used the horses for transporting material in his business. He was home in the evenings and sometimes for the noon meal. It was great to have him around all the time, like on the farm.

I immediately liked Rich Hill, a small town of about two thousand. The nice, natural swimming hole about two blocks from our house was a gathering place for the whole town. There was a new skating rink, a new bowling alley, and a movie theatre. Best of all, the war was over, and all my brothers were safely home. Mom could relax for the first time in over four years. What more could I want?

Our one-and-a-half story house was nice, but it needed renovation and redecorating. We had electricity but no plumbing, so no bathroom for several weeks until Daddy got the plumbing in place. I took charge of the much-needed papering of the living room, three bedrooms, and the kitchen-dining room. I had papered rooms in our old Victorian house in Winchester. I papered the living room and the bedrooms in our new house before school started in September.

It was a busy summer. I learned to skate and started working for the skating rink, putting on clamp-on skates for other skaters. I had time to skate and skated free. I went bowling and to the movies when I could afford it on my allowance from Mom and Daddy.

Mom had not met many people in Rich Hill because she didn't go out often. One day she and I were in the grocery store when a woman introduced herself to Mom. During the conversation, she told Mom that her only son, who had been in combat, was home on leave. Mom told the woman she had four sons in battle, and they all came back alive. Instead of expressing gratitude for Mom's good fortune, the woman said, "Well, if one of your sons had died, it wouldn't matter so much to you, because you still have three sons left."

For a moment, I thought Mom was going to attack the woman. I stepped between them. Then Mom said, in a firm voice, "Each of my sons is just as precious to me as your one son is to you!" I hurried Mom out of the store, and we walked home together. One of my brothers went back and bought the groceries.

Mom continued to cook her special main dishes and desserts but never used a written recipe. She kept them in her head. I wanted to learn to cook as well as she did. When I asked her what to put in the mix, she would say, "A pinch of this" or "A handful of that."

I decided I was going to learn to cook better than Mom. So, I started collecting recipes from family and friends. Mom allowed even encouraged me to use them. Even with the recipes, my cooking never turned out or tasted as good as her cooking.

That fall, I started high school. I checked out books from the school library for him and me to read. We both enjoyed historical novels, and after we both read the same book, we would discuss it. We also read and discussed the Bible. I was often doing homework, skating, and attending ball games at school. Daddy spent some time doing bookwork for his business, but we still made time to spend evenings together. He always treated me like a grown-up.

After a couple of years, Daddy built, remodeled, and restored many houses in the small town of about two thousand. There was no longer enough carpentry work to support the family. Unemployment was at a high level, with all the servicemen returning from the war looking for work.

A former boss Daddy had worked for during the war owned a construction company in Kansas City. The man persuaded Daddy to go there and work for his company in a management position. The pay was excellent, so Daddy took the job. But it was back to only seeing him on weekends because Kansas City was about seventy miles away. My brother, Fred, had quit school and went to work with him.

Mom became acquainted with a neighbor lady and started going with her to a doctor in the next town a few miles away. I don't know what the doctor's treatment was, but she seemed to be feeling better and more relaxed. That is, until....

One Saturday, I spent the day washing, hanging clothes, cleaning the house, and then dressed to go skating. I had walked a short distance when I heard and saw a car drive up in front of our home. A sheriff got out and walked to the front door. I hurried back to the house, and I heard him tell

Mom that Daddy had been in a car accident and was in the hospital about ten miles away. He came to take Mom to the hospital and told me I should stay at the house.

The date was October 11th, 1947. Two younger brothers and my sister were at home with me. My brother, Fred, was with Daddy in the accident. Mom said she would call when she had news, so I sat close to the phone.

After about half-an-hour, the phone rang. When I answered, the man's voice on the line said, "I'm so sorry to hear about your dad being killed in the car accident. I said, "No, he was only hurt and is in the hospital." The man hung up. Soon the phone started ringing non-stop. People were telling me how sorry they were that Daddy had died in the accident. After a while, I realized and accepted that it was true.

Mom had tried to call, but the phone was busy. The sheriff brought Mom and Fred back and walked her to the door. She was in such grief and shock that she went to bed and had me call her doctor to make a house call, which he did. She stayed in bed until the following Wednesday when we went to El Dorado Springs for the funeral service on Thursday.

I was the oldest of the kids at home, so I had to contact all our family members and friends. Fred and I were so traumatized we could hardly function, but we did what we had to do. I called my two brothers and families who lived about forty miles away in Cedar County. They came in a couple of hours. Other relatives started arriving, and by midnight the house was full of people talking and laughing about old times. I stepped outside to get away from the noise, but my older brother had me come back inside.

The following day the hospital called and said they needed someone to identify Daddy's body since neither Mom nor Fred had not done that. Someone came and took me to the hospital. They took me into a side room where Daddy's body was lying on a table. He was uncovered from his waist up. After being thrown from the car onto the pavement, his face was disfigured, but recognizable. I had never seen him without a shirt. I noticed his upper body and arms were a mass of muscles, a lingering memory for me. He was fifty-three years old.

I was responsible for making all the arrangements. Aunts, uncles, and cousins on both sides of the family were called about the tragic news. I called them again when we knew the date of the memorial service. Some lived in California and throughout the country and drove all the way.

I arranged with the funeral home in Rich Hill to prepare Daddy for the viewing and to transfer him by hearse Thursday morning to the church in El Dorado Springs. I contacted the church to arrange for the service, which my pastor, Brother Toppass, delivered. Finally, I arranged with the cemetery near El Dorado Springs, where Daddy would be buried, next to "Lil' Earl," to prepare the burial site.

It was so hectic! Phone calls came almost non-stop. Friends and neighbors brought lots of food, but I still had to cook with all our house guests, especially breakfast. Family members who came slept in their cars, on quilts on the floor, and some slept outside on pallets on the ground.

Wednesday afternoon, we drove to El Dorado Springs for the funeral service and burial on Thursday morning and stayed with relatives who lived there. I was grief-stricken and exhausted. One of my cousins was four years older than I was. We had been close friends since early childhood. Recognizing how upset I was, she tried to cheer me up. Not really understanding, she asked me to go out with her that evening, "It would make me feel better." I didn't go!

Thursday is a blur to me. I remember the sermon in the church, but I don't remember what was said. Walking by the coffin, I didn't look, knowing Daddy's face was disfigured on the viewing side. I recall being at the cemetery and the military service because Daddy was a World War I veteran.

I was relieved when we came back home Thursday afternoon because there were no house guests. Mom was up and about, not very strong and devastated. It was helpful to have peace and quiet. On Saturday, we did the laundry as usual. I was not ready, though, to go skating or to church on Sunday.

Mom wanted me to quit school and get a job, but I knew Daddy wanted me to graduate, and I wanted to finish school, too. Monday morning, I started back to school after being out for a week. The kids were surprised to see me, and most of them didn't know what to say. Before the school week was over, I caught up on my English, math, and science school work. And I continued with typing, music, and sports. It was helpful being settled back into school.

I was concerned for my brother, Fred. He was with Daddy in the accident. The car's wheels dropped off the highway's edge and caused the car to roll, throwing Daddy out of the car, causing a fatal head injury.

Fred was in the car and thrown into the back seat, which probably saved his life. It was a couple of weeks before Mom saw Fred's swollen left arm. He told her it had been swollen since the accident. When x-rayed, they found the break, and they put it in a cast. He removed the cast himself, later.

Mom was never the same. She did start going to church, which I had never known her to do in my lifetime. She was rebaptized and joined my church. In her young life, she had become a Christian. When she felt she had no choice but to get a divorce, they "Kicked her out of the church," and she could not attend. She could not have attended most churches when I was a child.

Mom had multiple decisions to make. She decided to move the family to El Dorado Springs, where my two older brothers could provide needed support for her. I stayed in Rich Hill to finish my senior year of high school.

I finished school at mid-term, then went to stay with Mom for a few weeks. My being there allowed Mom to visit her son and family in Wichita for a couple of weeks while I took care of my young siblings at home, giving Mom a much-needed break.

Recovery was slow in coming. All the family was grieving, too, especially Mom. She needed more help from me than ever. Finances were skimpy until a small amount if insurance came in. A brother in the army got an allotment for the family, but it was less than we needed. We didn't have much for extras.

Our lives changed forever with Daddy's passing. I shall always miss him and the positive influence and impact he had on my life.

WHITE CHRISTMAS

About a month before Christmas in 1941, when I was ten years old, my family moved from my childhood farm in Cedar County, Missouri, so we could all be closer to Daddy. He worked as a carpenter on building a military base near Joplin, Missouri. World War II had not yet started, but there were signs on the horizon.

A few days before we left the farm, our old speckled rooster woke me. I looked out the bedroom window. The sun was just coming up, and a new heavy blanket of snow had fallen in the night.

Snow covered the ground and piled high on the cedar trees and the birch's bare limbs, sycamore, hickory, and walnut trees. The sun shone on the glistening icicles hanging from the eves and the snow. It was more beautiful than the electric lights I saw in town a few years ago.

Daddy was home. He had been working away from home on defense work for several months and was not home often. He didn't have a car. My brothers were big enough to run the farm. The folks decided to sell the farm and move close to where he worked. They auctioned the animals and equipment, and they sold the farm.

Daddy then bought a used car and borrowed a truck to haul the furniture. With the boys helping, we loaded up and headed for Joplin and our new home. As we drove into Joplin, it was nighttime, and Christmas lights seemed to surround us, a wonderland.

We arrived at a big stone house that Daddy had rented in the country. And we had electricity for the first time. But the bad odor of the coal-burning stove was awful! On the farm, we burned wood, sometimes cedar, and it always smelled good. There was, however, a radio. I had never seen or heard one. Now I could listen to music all the time. Never mind we still had an outhouse and a well.

As the family listened to church music on the radio on Sunday morning, December 6, 1941, the newsman interrupted the program to say someone had bombed Pearl Harbor.

Instantly everything changed for the family and the country. I had one brother in the Navy, another a Medic in the Army, and three more married brothers eligible for the draft. I had never seen my folks more anxious and depressed. Mom was tearful much of the time, and I had nightmares and sleep-walked. These were the brothers that had carried me to school and looked out for me: they might die like the men at Pearl Harbor.

I had just started at our new school. It was crowded but nice. I didn't understand how it got heated because there were no stoves. There were four rooms, eight grades, and over one hundred students; about twenty-five students in each room. I soon missed my friends in the one-room school back home, with a heating stove, where I knew everyone, and everyone knew me. I had the same teacher for over five years. I knew no one except my four brothers at the new school and didn't see them often.

The other kids were mostly "city kids" and thought we talked funny. Their clothes were different, too; "store-bought." My brothers wore overalls, but Mom made my dresses from printed feed sacks on the treadle sewing machine. I thought they were "purdy." I noticed that in the bathrooms—I didn't know about bathrooms—that the other girls wore "store-bought" panties. They noticed that I wore flannel bloomers that Mom and I made. I was used to my friends back home liking my clothes; their clothes were about the same as mine.

The teacher in my crowded fifth and sixth-grade classroom was nice to me. As we were practicing for the Christmas program, she noticed that I knew the songs, which I learned from the radio and was singing out, even though I was so shy I would hardly talk. She asked me to sing a solo, "Up on the Housetop" in the program, and I did!

Because of my teacher back home, my big brothers, and Daddy teaching me math, I was ahead of most kids in my class in division and multiplication. The teacher had me help her work with the other kids. That helped some to make me become more accepted.

We had art classes which I loved and had never had before. But I was always drawing and coloring. Being told that all colors came from red, yellow, and blue was a revelation to me. I had to check it out before believing it. After much experimenting, yes, it was so!

There was a kitchen, and the cooks prepared hot lunches, another first for me. No more peanut butter and honey sandwiches. The cooks soon called me their "good eater." I wonder why?

One evening just before Christmas, I was listening to the radio and heard the beautiful song, "White Christmas." Bing Crosby was singing, "I'm dreaming of a white Christmas, just

like the ones I used to know, where the treetops glisten...."
Leaning back in the wooden rocking chair, I closed my eyes
and saw myself back on the farm, looking out the window at
that beautiful snow scene. I wanted to go back to the farm
for Christmas and be with my school friends and sing with
them.

We moved three more times during the war as Daddy felt
he needed to help to build military bases and defense plants.
The best part was they drafted two other brothers, and the
four brothers were in combat on the front lines for three or
four years. They all came back safely. Only one suffered a
minor injury after the war.

Even now, I never hear the song "White Christmas"
without going back to the beautiful scene etched in my
memory from my childhood of that morning on the farm
so many decades ago. There has never been a picture,
photograph or moving picture that can match that scene's
memory.

MY CHILDHOOD DREAMS

Tired of running and playing in the yard, I was lying in the cool grass on my back, watching the floating clouds and pretty birds in the clear blue sky. The birds were dipping, dashing, and floating about in the air. I wished I could fly like a bird in the sky.

Relaxed and half asleep, I heard a loud noise in the sky. I jumped up. So very scared. There was a big bird in the sky, making the loud noise. I ran to the house to find Mom, who was working in the kitchen, as she always was. When I told her what I saw and heard, she said it wasn't a bird. It was an airplane; I had never heard of an airplane. She said they have engines in them like our neighbor's truck and men fly in them.

In the sky, the airplane looked littler than I was. I wondered how a man could fly in something so little. Maybe they laid down on the airplane and held onto the wings. I thought I will fly like a bird in an airplane when I get big, not now when I'm just five years old.

A few days later, Daddy and the boys went fishing. They wouldn't let me go along because they said I was too little and couldn't keep up with them. I think it might have been because I was a girl. So, I decided I'd show them I could go fishing, too, by myself.

I tied a long piece of string to a long straight stick. Then I tied a nail to the other end of the string, using it for a fishhook, just like Daddy did. Sitting on the high side of the front porch floor, I hung my line and hook over the porch side and fished. It didn't matter that there was no water. Sitting there, I dreamed and thought and planned about what I would do when I get big.

I already knew what I wanted. I wanted my own house and my own husband. I wanted just four children, two boys, and two girls. I knew that I was plain looking with short, straight, brown hair and suntanned skin, not like some little girls who had blonde, curly hair, blue eyes, and pink skin. My husband would be good looking so I could have good looking kids. I had seen some men in the neighborhood that were not good looking, like Daddy. And my husband must own a candy store, so I could have all the candy I wanted and not have to share it with my brothers.

Also, I would be a nurse. An older brother was a Medic in the Army. He brought me a book that showed what we look like inside. Not knowing how to read, I just looked at the pictures. Fascinated and curious, I asked my brother what girls do where he works. He said they are called nurses, and they take care of sick people. I will be a nurse when I grow up.

A few years later, when I was ten, I started hearing grownups talking about the war across the "pond," and I was so scared. I knew Daddy and the boys shot animals for food, but I didn't know men shot each other. Soon, four of my brothers had to fight in the war.

Daddy said we had to sell the farm so he could work building army bases and ammunition plants for the war. I missed the farm, but there was so much to see and learn through the war years. We moved three times before the war was over. We had a car and a radio for the first time and sometimes electricity, running water, and a bathroom for the first time in my life. Best of all, when the war was over, all my brothers came home alive. So many others did not.

The summer they ended the war, we moved from a small town in Kansas to a small town in Missouri, where I started my freshman year of high school. My dream was still to become a nurse, a pilot, a wife, and a mother. But I would not get married until I was twenty-five years old.

NEVER GIVE UP

Growing up in the country and with so many brothers, I became athletic and strong. In our country school, all ages played workup softball, tag, and especially pump rope. At home, I jumped rope by myself and could jump hundreds of times without missing. I was still jumping rope in my seventies.

We moved to Winchester when I was twelve years old. All of us kids played basketball on outside courts and swam in farm ponds in the summer. That was where I learned to swim.

When I was thirteen, my brothers and their friends invited me to play football with them, playing quarterback. I was excited to be playing boys' games, but soon realized I was the one who always got tackled. My excitement faded, and I stopped playing football.

By the summer we moved to Rich Hill when I was fourteen, people called me stocky. I didn't like that. In my bathing suit, I looked like a muscled Olympic gymnast.

A former rock quarry pond with crystal clear water, with shallow and deep sides, was a couple of blocks from our house. It was a favorite gathering place for the towns' kids. I went swimming most days that summer and could swim many laps without stopping, outdoing most of the boys, which was my favorite thing.

That summer, a new skating rink opened in the town. I learned to roller-skate, but only after much effort. Mom bought me a new brown cotton slack suit for skating. At first, I fell a lot, and the suit was covered with dust and had to be washed each time. Eventually, I learned to skate well and was doing "tricks" with the best of them.

I became a "skate girl" to pay for my admission and get the first choice to wear a pair of shoe skates. Then I could skate the three nights a week when the rink was open. Most skates were "clamp- ons'" to regular shoes. My job was to fit them to the kids' own shoes. I got to know most of the kids and young people in town.

There were about 200 students during my freshman year. But only a few new ones in our four-year high school. The teachers were welcoming to us, the other students …. not so much.

The girls' basketball team was forming. I was the new girl they didn't know. Being five feet and a half-inch tall, I was the shortest girl. Most of them were six to ten inches taller than me.

But I was a good "shooter." Born left-handed, my teacher and family made me change to writing with my right hand. They couldn't make me change, though, to my right hand to throw a ball. I always threw with my left hand. I didn't know it then but found out years later that I'm Dyslexic, as many good, even great, athletes are. Dyslexia is considered a gift … so they say.

Girls' basketball practice was the period after lunch. I went alone to the gym during lunchtime and practiced shooting, instead of eating lunch. Our school lunches were 20 cents a day, $1.00 a week. I saved my dollar for other things.

I never told Mom I wasn't eating lunch, but she did wonder why I was so hungry when I got home from school. I made peanut butter sandwiches and ate any leftovers but was ready to eat supper a couple of hours later.

Girls' basketball had a First and Second Team. Both teams played on the same evening, so we all got a chance to play. I played full time on the second team, which played first and substituted on the first team. This allowed me to get free rides and admission to the games, in and out of town.

Being so short, I couldn't play guard, so I played forward. At that time, girls' basketball regulations only allowed them to play half-court. The forwards on one team played on one half of the court, and the guards on the other team played that half-court to guard the forwards. The set-up was reversed on the opposite side. No players crossed the center line. The regulation was in effect for many years before being discontinued.

In addition, women, girls, and small kids could not double dribble. Only a single dribble was allowed at the time I played. The forwards stood at the center line, waiting for our team's guards to throw the ball to us.

My legs were short, but I could run fast. When someone threw a ball to me, I quickly turned and bounced it once, several feet ahead of the other players and me. Running fast, I caught the ball and made a basket. Sometimes, the other team's big guards would run toward me, thinking I would move out of their way. I took a stance, and when they ran into me and fouled me, I got free throws, which I made almost 100% of the time. My practice paid off.

The first team's inner circle had their favorite friends and would play better with them in practice and not so well with me. I was not one of them, nor did I want to be. I didn't make the first team. But in competition, when someone on our team fouled out, they played fine with me. This was the first time I experienced "cliques," but not the last.

I accepted the way it was and made the most of it. I knew I was not the best player, mostly because of my size. I played often and believed I helped the team become one of the best teams in the district. They were usually in First place.

I lettered in basketball, playing on the first team, playing as a sub for two years, and wore the girls' pretty basketball uniform at the games.

One of the senior girls on the basketball team became a friend. She was the majorette for our marching band. I played the bass drum. She would tell students in the band to follow my drumbeat. She was the only child of a wealthy older couple. They owned businesses in town, and her mother always drove a limousine.

She and I only had contact in school activities and were both in the drama classes, but we did different things. I liked memorizing humorous readings, humorous and serious poetry. My friend did debate and extemporaneous speaking.

In late winter of my freshman year, there was going to be a Drama Event for district high schools, for all students who wished to participate. Students were awarded a One, Two, or Three rating for the quality of their performance. It was not a competition, and each student could rate a "One" if they qualified.

The event was twenty miles away, but I had no way to go. My friend invited me to ride with her and her mother in their limousine. It was a cold, wintry day. I walked several blocks in the morning to their business. They invited me to sit in the back seat for the ride. When we arrived, she went to her events, and I went to mine.

There were many students there. I did my memorized humorous reading and poems throughout the morning, while my friend performed in her chosen area. It the end, I was pleased to have gotten a "One" rating on all three of my performances.

When the event was over, my friend came and said we were going home. She was upset and told me she received a "Three" rating on both her Debates and Extemporaneous Speaking. As I sat in the back seat, I noticed her mother was angry.

As we started home, her mother said, "It's too bad that someone with no talent at all could get 'One' ratings, but someone really talented gets a' Three' rating." My friend just looked straight ahead. We rode the twenty miles home in silence.

When we arrived in town, I quickly jumped out of the car and ran home in the shivering cold weather. "Oh! I forgot to thank my friend's mother for the ride!" I remained friends with her, but it was never the same between us.

When I started my sophomore year, we had a new English teacher, Mrs. Pfost. She noticed that I knew the parts of speech and sentence structure in my writing assignments. In the spring, she encouraged me to enter a speech writing contest coming up soon.

It was not long after World War II ended, and veterans were appreciated and being honored. The American Legion was active in the area, including many local farmers. They were sponsoring a patriotic speech writing contest among high school students. After submission, the speech was to be memorized and given by the student in open competition. Each speech was several minutes long.

Only one other girl in my class and I entered written speeches. We memorized the speeches and prepared to give them before American Legion judges in a school assembly early one afternoon.

I wore my usual casual school clothes. The other girl's mother came to our school during lunch hour. She brought dress clothes for her daughter, styled her hair, and helped her with her makeup. I combed and styled my own hair.

The students assembled in one large room. The judges were friends of the girl's father, who was also a member of the American Legion. I don't recall who went first, but we each took turns standing before the judges and students and gave our memorized speeches.

The three judges entered into a discussion for a few minutes. They turned and awarded the other girl First Place and awarded me Second Place. But it wasn't over....

The following fall, the American Legion announced a regional contest for Patriotic speeches from many schools. The contest was many miles away. I don't recall how I got there, but I went and competed. So did the other girl. I won first place, but I never heard how she placed. She didn't seem to want to tell me.

Lessons Learned: Never give up! You may not win, but you know you did your very best!

SCHOOL DAYS AND CHURCH

When we started school in Joplin, Missouri, it was like we had moved to a foreign country. We talked a different language, "Hillbilly." I tried to "talk proper" like my teacher but was not very successful.

The four-room country school was over-crowded with about hundred students. It had a gymnasium and an auditorium. Best of all, there was a kitchen and cooks that prepared hot lunches.

We rode a bus to school, and the six of us kids were first to get on the bus at 6:45. By the time we got to school, the bus was packed with students of all ages, sitting double in the seats and standing in the isles. When the bus stopped at the school, the kids ran inside, and I was left alone in the schoolyard.

As I ventured inside, kids were moving in every direction into classrooms. Not knowing where to go, I was alone again. A teacher asked what grade I was in and took me to the art room where they gave me paper and crayons to draw pictures. I started to relax and enjoy drawing when a loud clanging buzzer sounded. The kids jumped up and ran out of the room. I had heard about air raid warnings and thought there was an air raid coming. It was the school bell. I had never heard one before, and I ran into the hallway. Kids were moving in every direction. As I stood alone, panicked, the same teacher came by and took me to a classroom.

Gradually I won favor with my teacher. I was in the fifth

grade, but ahead of many math students, even the sixth graders because Daddy and my brothers taught me. The teacher had me working with other students, helping her teach long division and multiplication. I had memorized my multiplication tables.

The next fall, Daddy was recruited to do essential defense work near Lawrence, Kansas. Because housing was scarce near Lawrence, he rented a house in Winchester, a small town with about two hundred population.

Starting to another school was misery. Still shy, I walked the two blocks to school, and not knowing where to go, I sat down in a swing on the playground. The bell rang, and a girl about my age came out and took me inside. My room had the sixth, seventh and eighth grades. I was in the sixth grade.

There was a teacher shortage due to the war. My teacher, Miss Young, had been retired but came back to teach. She was an excellent teacher, the best I had since leaving the farm. There were usually about fifteen students in the room the three years I was there. I liked the school and had many new and pleasant experiences.

A few days after starting, Miss Young had us take a True/False test. It didn't count on our grades. The test was new then, at least in that area, and we were doing it for the first time. Of the three classes, I was the only one who passed the test, missing only a few questions. It seemed to get the teacher's attention and gave me a good start.

I was in Miss Young's classroom all the time we lived in Winchester. She seemed impressed that I memorized quickly. She noticed I liked grammar and memorized the parts of speech and the parts of the sentence. I knew how to use a protractor and compass better than some older students. So, she had me working with her, helping them. Once again, Daddy and my brothers had taught me.

I graduated from the eighth grade in Winchester. That summer, the combat of war was over. With Daddy's work finished in Lawrence, we sold our house there and moved in June to Rich Hill, Missouri.

A schoolteacher gave me private speech lessons in her home in the summertime for twenty-five cents. I started lessons, hoping it would help me with my "hillbilly" accent, which I had not completely lost. She had me memorize poems and humorous readings and arranged for me to perform before community groups. What she taught me was helpful when I started high school.

A prominent businessman in town owned a school bus and drove a route for the school. He had established a Drum and Bugle Corps not connected to the school made up of about twenty high school girls. When I saw them marching in a parade in their pretty uniforms, I asked to join the corps but didn't know how to play the drum or a bugle. About half of the girls carried bugles but didn't know how to play them. The other girls played snare drums, but no one played the bass drum. I joined and learned how to play the bass drum.

We marched in parades, usually on Saturday. That fall, the director arranged for us to march in Ringling Brothers Circus in Kansas City: "The Greatest Show on Earth." Early one Saturday, we donned our uniforms and rode the bus to Kansas City. We marched in the parade before the circus started and stayed to watch the performance before returning home. It was the most incredible fun I ever experienced, and it was free!

Starting at a new school is always a challenge, and this would be the fifth one in the last four years. There are always bullies and cliques that shut out a new student. I was making my clothes and altering hand-me-downs. They didn't usually look like the other girls' clothes. I didn't care; I was pleased that I made them. Ever since leaving the farm, I was often ridiculed.

Our school day had nine class-periods of forty-five minutes each. We took six classes and used three periods for study hall. I did that the first semester, but the remaining semesters I usually took nine subjects, including glee club, band, orchestra, and sports. After helping Mom, I studied at home in the evening, often studying until midnight or later.

Because I learned to play the drums, I joined the pep club band and marching band. I played in the marching band for football games and the pep-club band for basketball games at home and neighboring towns. Which meant I attended the games for free. Otherwise, I could not have gone to the games.

We started girls' basketball practice when school started. I was five feet and one-half inch. Most of the girls were much taller. I didn't make the first team but was one of the first substitutes. We had second-team games, then first-team games, back-to-back, the same evening. I played full time on the second team, which allowed me to go to all the games, in and out of town, free!

I became acquainted with Beth, a girl in my class. She invited me to her church. For some reason, I told her I was going to another church, which I wasn't. She remained friendly and often invited me to church. I'd say I would go and then didn't.

One Friday, Beth invited me to church on Sunday, and I promised her I would, but I didn't. Monday, when I saw her, she sounded disappointed and said, "I was hoping to see you at church yesterday." Surprised that she cared so much, I promised to go the next Sunday, and I did.

I liked the small church and started going Sunday mornings, then Sunday and Wednesday evenings. The members of the congregation made me feel welcome. Beth's father was the pastor, and her mother played the piano. Her family often invited me to their home for Sunday dinner. We visited, played games, and sometimes took walks in the afternoon, then attended the evening church services.

In the fall, when I was fifteen and a half, I had taken on a lot of responsibility of my choosing—I wanted to do it all. Besides the heavy school schedule, I helped Mom with cooking, cleaning, and other chores. It was tiring, but I kept the busy schedule.

As I attended church, the sermons and Bible studies gripped my attention. At one Sunday evening service, the pastor referred us to Mathew 11: 28-29 (KJV) and read the verses: "Come unto me all ye who labor and are heavy laden and I will give you rest. Take my yoke upon you and learn of me for I am meek and lowly in heart, and ye shall find rest for your souls."

When the pastor explained the meaning of the verses, it was just what I needed to hear. I decided to accept Jesus' promise, follow Him, and find rest. As the congregation sang the invitation song, those who decided to follow Jesus stepped out and went to the front. At first, I hesitated, then I went forward. At the close of the hymn, the church members came by, shaking my hand and, yes, sometimes hugging me.

The following Sunday evening, I was baptized by emersion in the church baptistry. I remember the words of the song the congregation sang: "Ring the bells of Heaven, there is joy today, for a soul departed from the foe."

Later, when I told Mom and Daddy of my decision and that they baptized me, Mom was pleased. Daddy said, "That's good! I just hope you stick with it." He had known friends and family members that did not "Stick with it."

Life was becoming less stressful by the end of my freshman year. I made friends with many of the kids and enjoyed the summer. With a break from school, I skated often and spent many happy hours at the swimming hole.

I started my Sophomore year, still carrying a full schedule. The girls' basketball team was involved in a tournament. We had a game on Saturday. I told the coach I couldn't go because I helped Mom do the laundry that day. He said, "We need you. Ask your Mom if you can go." When I asked her, she said, "Sure! You go, the boys can help me one time." I went.

The spring semester started, and my sixteenth birthday was March 2nd. One Sunday morning at church, a girlfriend told me about some guys she met the night before at the skating rink. They wanted to meet some girls. I told her I wasn't interested. I had never dated because I didn't want to date.

Soon after this, my life changed in many ways.

A CHRISTMAS GIFT

The summer I was fourteen years old, my family moved to Rich Hill, Missouri, where I started high school. Daddy worked as a foreman for a construction company in Kansas City. Because of the work being seventy miles away, he could only be home on weekends.

I missed Daddy not being home all the time as he was on the farm. I remember him there reading The *Weekly Kansas City Star*, farming journals, and often the Bible in the evening by lamplight. When he came home on weekends, he and I often spent an evening talking about news, politics, history, and the Bible. I would check out books from the school library, read them, and then he would take them with him to read during the week. He would bring them back the next weekend when we would discuss them.

When we moved to Rich Hill, I started going to church. In the fall of my sophomore year, I decided one Sunday morning to accept Christ into my life and to follow him. They baptized me that evening. When I told Mom and Daddy that I had been baptized, Daddy looked thoughtful, then said, "That's good! I just hope you stick with it."

As we often did, Daddy and I spent one Saturday evening discussing the books he had read during the week. Soon our conversation turned to talk about the Bible. I asked Daddy what he believed about going to Heaven. He said, "I'm not sure. How do you believe we get to Heaven?"

Fumbling for words and unsure how to answer, I said, "You just have to be saved."

He answered, "I don't know how to be saved."

Still unsure how to express myself, I stammered, "You just have to believe that God sent Jesus to save us and then follow Him." We dropped the discussion, and soon we discussed the books he had taken with him the past week.

The following weekend, October 11th, Daddy was on the way back from Kansas City. About ten miles from home, he died in a single-car, roll-over accident in which he was driving. He was thrown out of the car. The report said that he died instantly. His accident and death were and is the greatest tragedy and loss of my entire life.

Mom wanted me to quit school and go to work. I was sixteen and in my junior year of school. I wanted to finish school, and I knew Daddy had wanted me to finish school. Mom had a small amount of life insurance, and somehow the family managed to get through the winter.

I had met Bill just a few months before the accident. He became my greatest emotional support and offered to marry me. But we would have to live in motels because the Missouri State paint crew he worked with moved often. When I told him I wanted to finish school, he agreed that would be best. Besides, at just sixteen, I knew I wasn't ready for marriage. I made it through the school year with the help of family, friends, and teachers.

The following summer, between my junior and senior years in high school, I went to Kansas City to stay with a relative and got a job with a mail-order company. While I was at Kansas City that summer, Mom moved from Rich Hill to El Dorado Springs, Missouri, about forty miles away.

When it was time for school to start, I wanted to finish

high school in Rich Hill. Bill made it possible by paying my room and board. I moved in and started to school. When I realized the cost for him was too much to continue, I looked for another arrangement. That one didn't work out, so I found another one, actually two: as a maid and a waitress. My boss allowed me to put school first and I studied in my room late at night. I managed to finish my senior year at mid-term, in January, on the Honor Roll.

Still very much grieving the loss of Daddy and with the stress and hard work of the past many months wearing on me, I was exhausted most of the time. Ever since he died, I could not get the memory out of my mind of him, saying, "I don't know how to be saved," the last time we talked. I often wondered if how I answered was helpful for him.

One Saturday night, just before Christmas, after doing laundry, cleaning the house, and working three meals in the restaurant, I collapsed into bed. Exhausted, I fell into a deep sleep. Soon I was back in the restaurant, behind the counter, wiping the countertops. There didn't seem to be anyone else around. Then I heard someone and looked up. Daddy was sitting on the stool on the other side of the counter, smiling as usual. I was bewildered and amazed, but so thankful and happy.

At first, I was speechless! Then I said, "How did you get here?"

Smiling, he said quietly, "I just thought I'd come down and see you for a while."

I awakened, and realizing I had been dreaming, I sat straight up in bed! Peace and joy flooded my being. It had lifted such a weight off my shoulders I felt like I could float.

The dream is as real as anything that has ever happened

in my life. I believe God sent me a message through a dream: Daddy is waiting for me in Heaven. God revealed to Daddy how to get to Heaven and that Daddy believed and accepted God's promise before he died. This I Believe!

What a Wonderful Christmas Gift!

AN OLD HEAD ON YOUNG SHOULDERS

My high school's annual picture album, "THE TIGER," was coming out in the spring. Having finished school at mid-term, I was impatiently waiting at Mom's for it to come in the mail.

When it finally came, I enjoyed looking at my Senior classmates' pictures, which I had not previously seen. Most of the pictures were surprisingly attractive. My classmates looked so mature and grown-up.

They all had a nickname: Giggles, Dimples, Red, to name a few. As I noticed my picture, I was surprised to see the nickname "Moe." A guy had given me the nickname a couple of years before when I cut my bangs. The look reminded him of "Moe" in the Three Stooges, a comedy team at the time. I had hoped they had forgotten the nickname. Not!

Beside each student's picture was a list of their accomplishments. My list of eight activities included music, sports, and drama.

There were "Quips" beside all the pictures. Some of those by girls' names were, "She knows not of her charms," "Her friends are numbered among the stars," and "Her brown eyes say things that her lips dare not utter."

I had never heard the quip by my name, and it jumped out at me, "An old head on young shoulders." I was surprised and really didn't like it. But I suppose the classmates who put the yearbook together knew how hard I worked under challenging circumstances to finish high school when I could have taken the easy way out and quit.

Eventually, I came to appreciate the "Quip."

Bonnie Lacey, senior

AND SO IT BEGINS

The day I met Bill was the best day of my life. My whole world was about to change.

He worked for the State Highway Department with a crew painting bridges along the west side of Missouri, south to north. They moved up the highway every few weeks to paint the next bridge.

While he was in Wichita for about a month, we went skating, bowling, and to the movies. And I took my first airplane ride. When it was raining, the crew couldn't work. As I stepped out of our front door, Bill was there waiting in his car to take me to school. And he waited in front of the school to take me home at the end of the day.

He was so quiet, but so much fun and so nice, not rowdy like my brothers. Also, I had had no one pay my way before. That was nice, and he was so handsome. I didn't realize it then, but it was a good start on the dream I'd had as a child of a good-looking husband, so we could have good-looking children because I thought I was plain-looking.

When the paint crew moved on, Bill returned in a month to see me and stayed in the hotel. We went skating and to church and spent Sunday afternoon together. He always left me the hotel's phone where he stayed out of town, and we often wrote letters. Before the summer was over, he was coming back about every other weekend. He worked half-days on Saturdays, so he was usually late in the evening for his visit.

By the time I started my junior year in the fall, we were committed to getting married when I graduated from high school. He continued visiting every other weekend, sometimes traveling over one hundred miles at thirty-five miles an hour, the average speed limit then.

On Saturday, October 11, 1947, my life took another tragic change, and Bill was not in town. A sheriff came to my family's house and told Mom that Daddy had been in a car accident. I didn't learn until later that he had died in the roll-over accident. As the oldest of the kids at home, and with Mom barely able to function, many difficult tasks fell to me. I desperately needed Bill.

I called the hotel number he had given me. A man answered and said Bill had left and didn't leave a number where I could reach him. I was shocked! I assumed he didn't want to see me or hear from me again. Another loss, the two most important people in my life were gone.

By the time the arrangements had been made, and we got through the funeral service, I was grief-stricken and exhausted. I was relieved when the houseguests left, and there was peace and quiet at home.

Not being able to contact Bill was always on my mind. We had made so many plans for our future when I graduated from high school. I could not yet forget the plans and Bill.

Mom wanted me to quit school and get a job, but I knew Daddy wanted me to graduate, and I wanted to finish school, too. I started back to school after being out for a week. The kids were surprised to see me, and most of them didn't know what to say. Before the school week was over, I caught up on my English, math, and science schoolwork. And I continued with typing, music, and sports. It was helpful being settled back in school.

On a Friday evening, three weeks after Daddy's accident, I dressed in my uniform to march with the band at a school football game. No one else played the bass drum. As I stepped out the front door, I saw Bill driving up in front of the house in his 1937 Hudson coupe. I ran to the passenger door and slid in. I could see he had lost weight and was very pale. (Many years later, I overheard Bill tell someone. 'I drove up in front of the house and saw Bonnie come running out in her 'Monkey Suit.')

Bill told me he had developed lead poisoning. The state used red lead paint as the base coat to paint the bridges. He became sick and went home to Freeburg, Missouri, to be treated by his family's doctor. He was sick in bed, too sick to write to me. His family didn't have a phone.

His older sister worked in Jefferson City, close to Freeburg, and she saw Daddy's obituary in the *Kansas City Star* newspaper. She had heard Bill talk about Rich hill and me. The next time she came home, she asked Bill if he knew who Herbert Lewis Lacey was.

When he heard the news, Bill said he decided immediately to see me, even though he was almost too sick to walk. His dad asked him, "Who is this girl? She must be pretty special!" Bill showed his dad the snapshot I had given him, taken on my sixteenth birthday. His dad looked at the picture and said, "You'd better go!" Bill drove over a hundred-fifty miles to get to my house.

Having him there and knowing we would continue our plans was the gift I needed. I told him the band was depending on me to play the bass drum that night.

He said, "That's alright. I need to check into the hotel and rest."

We visited for a while, and then he took me to school, where I marched with the band. He checked into the hotel, and I didn't see him again that night, but I knew he was nearby.

The next morning when I walked out the door to go to church, Bill was waiting in his car to take me there. He didn't go to church but was waiting for me when the service was over. We went to lunch and had a couple of hours to visit and, yes, cuddle.

Before he left to go back home to continue recovery, Bill offered to marry me then, if I wanted. When I told him that I wanted to finish school, he said that would be best. We would have had to live in hotels and eat in restaurants.

I was now more able to start my recovery after Bill's visit.

It was wintertime when Bill was well enough to return to work. The crew was working in southern Missouri, so we only saw each other every three or four weeks. I stayed involved in school and church activities and skated as often as possible, but I missed him being there to skate with me.

Winter seemed long and hard, but Bill's paint crew was moving closer with spring coming on. He came every other weekend or more. By the time spring came and the semester ended, his crew was working near Kansas City.

I was good friends with Ruth, the ex-wife of a cousin. She lived in Kansas City. She had two small children and invited me to stay with her for the summer and find work there. I would help her with housework and the children for room and board. Oh yes, Bill would be working in the Kansas City area that summer.

It was a good, yes, even a great summer. I got a job with a mail-order company and rode the bus to work. Ruth appreciated my "occasional" help with her children and the housework. Bill and I saw each other every weekend and sometimes in between. I began to relax and enjoy life, but I still missed Daddy.

Changes were happening back in Rich Hill. That summer, Mom sold our house and moved to El Dorado Springs to be near my two older brothers and their families. That left me with choices to make. Was I going to El Dorado Springs to finish high school? Or was it possible for me to stay in Rich Hill and finish high school there?

Bill helped me solve the dilemma. One weekend we drove to Rich Hill from Kansas City. I knew of a woman there who rented rooms to students. She charged $5.00 a week for room and board, a lot of money at that time. Bill managed his money well and had some savings. He offered, even insisted, that I take the room. What a relief to know I could finish school in Rich Hill. When I started school, I expected to be there until spring. I quickly realized that the room's cost was too much of a burden for Bill, even though he didn't seem to mind.

I heard about a well-to-do couple who had twin girls and a new baby girl. They wanted someone to live with them, help care for the girls, help with housework for room and board, and I could go to school. The first of October I moved there. Soon after moving in, they wanted me to quit school and work for them full time. I began looking for another place to live.

A woman who owned a large house and rented rooms to men needed help with laundry and cleaning. She had a live-in maid's room and offered it to me, I accepted. She also owned the best restaurant in town. She said I could work there for my meals when not in school. I accepted and moved in the first week of November.

She was supportive and encouraged me to put school first and to go to church. She allowed me time to be with Bill when he was in town, usually every weekend. He stayed in the hotel next to the restaurant and ate his meals there while I was working. I was usually tired, but all was going smoothly.

It started to get cold. Bill noticed my winter coat was old and worn, a hand-me-down. He suggested we go to a town close by where there was a large clothing store and buy me a new coat. One Saturday afternoon, we drove to the store. Several coats were brought out for me to try on. There was a beautiful gray, hooded coat that I really liked.

When I tried on other coats, there was a brightly colored plaid one. I looked at all the price tags of all the coats as I tried them on. The plaid coat's price was $15.00, and the gray coat cost $35.00. I told Bill I wanted the plaid coat, but he said, "No, we'll take the gray one." He liked the gray coat best and knew I liked it. He didn't like gaudy colors like the plaid coat. But $35.00 was a fortune then, more than a weeks' wages. It was a good investment, though, because I wore it for many years, long after we were married.

Near the end of the semester, I realized I had enough credit hours to finish school at mid-term, a tremendous gift. All the hard work had paid off. When the semester ended in mid-January, I left Rich Hill to live with Mom in El Dorado

Springs. Bill visited me there every weekend.

We began making plans for our life together and set our wedding date for May 14. Bill was concerned about us living in hotels and having to eat out all the time. His newly married boss bought a camper-travel trailer to have their own home as they followed his work. Bill decided to find a used camper for us, which he could afford. He had some savings, but the trailers were rare and much in demand.

In February, Bill found a used camper he wanted, but the price was more than his savings. He borrowed $200 from his dad and promised to pay him back in a few months. But when he tried to pay him, his Dad said, "No, keep it for a wedding present." Bill parked the camper in Mom's yard, and he slept in it when he visited me on weekends.

By early April, the paint crew was working near North Kansas City and would be there all summer. Bill pulled the camper there, parked it, and lived in it, where we would live after we were married. In April, I moved back to Kansas City, worked for the mail-order company, and stayed with Ruth.

Bill and I went back to Rich Hill for my high school graduation on a Thursday evening. May 19th. We were married, though, the Saturday before on May 14th in Rich Hill. I had grown up.

Bill Krenning

Bonnie and Bill

Bill with camper

DEAR BILL, I LOVE YOU

Because you represent to me all that God expects a husband to be.

Because you are a wonderful, giving father to our children.

Because you are more concerned for me than you are for yourself.

Because you sometimes understand me better than I understand myself.

Because you are always there for me.

Because you encourage me in the things I try to do.

Because you are not afraid to tell me when I am wrong.

Because you like and accept me as I am.

Because you tolerate, even accept and love my family.

Because you were so good to my Mother.

Because you are my best friend.

Because of the secrets we share.

Because you love me.

Because you are God's gift to me.

Because you stopped, with my friends, and picked me up that Sunday afternoon on March 15th, so many years ago.

Love Always, Bonnie

MY CHRISTMAS TREES

When I was five years old, I saw my first Christmas tree in my one-room country school in Cedar County, Missouri. In that community, usually, only schools and churches had Christmas trees. And there were no churches close enough for us to attend by team and wagon.

I thought the tree was beautiful, so when I got home, I asked Daddy if we could have a Christmas tree. The next day he took me out to the pasture and cut a tree for my brothers and me. There were no electric lights, but my brothers and I made decorations and hung them. In my mind now, it was the most beautiful of all our Christmas trees over the decades.

Eventually, I grew up, mostly. Bill and I married in May after I finished high school. He worked for the Missouri State Highway Department with a group of men painting bridges. He was the only married man, besides the boss. The job usually entailed moving every two to four weeks throughout the state's middle and west side. The men, except the boss, stayed in hotels.

So, just before we married, Bill bought a used travel-trailer, a camper. He was the only man on the crew that owned a camper beside the boss.

I thought it was a castle with a beautiful plywood paneling, a domed ceiling, and kitchen built-ins. The front room measured seven by nine feet and had a sofa and a desk. It was plenty of space for us. I'm giving you these dimensions for a reason.

In August, we moved from Kansas City to Boonville, Missouri, to paint a large bridge over the Missouri River, and we stayed there until after Christmas.

I settled into my dream world of being a housewife. I ordered many household items from the Sears Roebuck catalog; and some clothing. Then, in early November, I received a Christmas catalog from the Roebucker as we called it, and I started looking, dreaming, and even planning on a Christmas tree and ordering decorations.

Then Bill's family invited us to their home, which was about an hour's drive away from where we lived for Thanksgiving Dinner. They lived in the country and had Cedar trees, considered a nuisance, growing in the pasture. I asked Bill if we could get a Christmas tree while we were there. He looked at me quizzically, his dimples deepening, and said, "Where will we put it?" Then he said, "Oh, I guess so."

After Thanksgiving dinner, Bill and his dad went out in the pasture and cut a six-food Cedar tree and loaded it into the trunk of our '37 Chevy coupe. When we got home, Bill made a stand and fastened the tree to it. It nearly touched the ceiling and, since it was a bushy Cedar, it spread out over four feet and filled two-thirds of the double doorway. We had to slide by it sideways.

Unknown to Bill, but because he had told me he would get the tree, I had ordered Christmas decorations and stored them in my closet. He put the lights up for me; the first time I had tree lights, and I finished the decorating. He didn't show his excitement like I did, but he made sure all the other men, including the boss and his wife, came over to see the tree.

Our first tree and the ritual have continued since I was five years old with a live tree over the decades. I sometimes thought we should have taken pictures of our first Christmas tree, Bill and mine. He had a camera. But maybe what I remember is better than the black and white photos would show.

A WHITE-KNUCKLED PASSENGER

On a beautiful Sunday afternoon, about a month after Bill and I met in March, we were out riding in his 1931 Model A with the windows rolled down. Two of his bridge painting buddies were in the back seat. Bill was the only one who had a car, besides the boss, so the guys were often in our company. As we drove into the countryside, we heard the engine noise and saw a small airplane flying low in the sky.

After watching for a while, I said, "I always wanted to fly in an airplane, ever since I was a little girl, and I saw my first plane flying like a bird in the sky." After a few moments, Bill said, "Well, now is as good a day as any." He surprised me by turning the car around and heading toward the highway.

An airport was about 20 miles away that gave rides on Sunday afternoon in an open cockpit, low-wing, single-engine plane. When we arrived at the airport, Bill and I got out of the car; the guys slowly got out. They were captive passengers, I guess. The guys urged me to go first because I was a girl, pretending to be polite. I suspect they weren't as eager to fly as I was. Bill paid two dollars for my ride; a lot of money in 1947, but I wasn't about to not go since he offered.

As I walked with the pilot toward the plane, I noticed that he was grinning. I saw no other women or girls there. He probably didn't have many female passengers, especially as young as I was; sixteen. He may also have worried about me becoming scared after we got up in the air.

We settled into the seats and took off, climbed up, then leveled. As I looked out, it seemed like we sat still. I leaned my head over the side of the plane. The wind hit me in the face so hard it jerked my head back. As I pulled my head back into the plane, I looked up front, and the pilot laughed. I smiled back. I guess he decided I wasn't afraid, so he climbed, doing small dives, and flying in circles on one side, then the other. It was such a thrill for me on my first ride. Bill and the guys all took short rides because, I think, they didn't want a girl showing them up. Then Bill took pictures of me beside the plane. As we headed back home, I couldn't believe what had happened.

It was many years later before I flew again. After we reared our four children, I started to Wichita State and graduated with my nursing degree at 48 years. Bill bought me a Cessna 150 for a graduation present. At age 50, I earned my pilot's license.

The grandkids soon expected me to take them up for short rides. They may have thought all Grandmas took their grandkids flying. I also loved doing stalls, so I would up by myself and fly around like a bird as I had dreamed as a child of five years. Also, Bill and I flew down to the Oklahoma City Airport and did several touch-and-goes before we headed back home.

Bill was a white-knuckle passenger. Especially with me. Nevertheless, he wanted to fly to the Jefferson City Airport near where he grew up. We landed and visited his nearby family. Then we flew over the family farm, about 50 miles away, circled over a few times, and headed back home.

Bill wasn't as air worthy as I and decided not to get his license. I started my master's degree in nursing, so we sold the plane after a few years, but that was all right. My childhood dreams came true, and many, many more!

YOU ALWAYS WUS A SCHEMER

I met Bill two weeks after my sixteenth birthday, March 2. My seventeenth birthday was coming up soon. Bill and I "knew" we would be married when I finished high school but had not announced it to anyone.

Bill worked out of town with a crew, painting bridges for the state, and visiting me most weekends. About a month before my birthday, he asked me if I wanted an engagement ring or a watch for my birthday.

Most of my friends at school knew how serious we were about each other, but I wasn't ready to wear an engagement ring at school yet. Then I remembered how Mom had always wanted a watch but never got one.

I considered the matter. *If I get a ring now, I may never get a watch. But if Bill gives me a watch for my birthday, I will probably get a ring from him later.* So, I answered, "I'd like a watch."

He asked me if I wanted a sports watch, knowing how "rowdy" I was. I said, "No."

The weekend before my birthday, Bill brought me a beautiful, tiny wristwatch. At the time, the advertising said a watch should be small enough to slide through your ring. This watch was small enough.

He slipped the watch on my wrist. It had a pretty beveled crystal glass front. Then he reached into his pocket and handed me the guarantee and the sale bill for me to keep. I saw the watch had a fourteen-carat gold case and had seventeen jewel works, about as good as you could get.

I noticed the price on the bill: $23.00. Bill's wages were $12.00 a week, plus expenses. He had spent two paychecks on my watch. Maybe I should have said "Yes" to the offer of a sports watch.

Within two weeks, I broke the beveled glass crystal on the watch and had to replace it with a plain glass crystal.

The watch was a good investment, though. It is still running and will be running for my ninetieth birthday. And I did get my engagement ring for my eighteenth birthday.

Many years later, I was telling someone about why I wanted a watch first. Bill was listening. With his dimples deepening, smiling inside, he quietly said, "You always wus a schemer!"

THE RING CAME IN THE MAIL

My eighteenth birthday was coming soon, and anticipation filled me. So many changes in my lie ahead.

I finished high school at midterm and was living with Mom at El Dorado Springs. Bill parked the camper he bought for us in her yard and stayed in it on his weekend visits.

Bill promised me an engagement ring for my birthday. One weekend he asked me if I wanted to go shopping for my ring. It just so happened I had been looking at rings in Mom's Sears and Roebuck Catalog. I showed him a certain ring I liked. It had a quarter carat diamond set in a white gold heart on an ornate yellow gold band, with a matching wedding ring. The price was $35.00.

He liked it, too, and filled out the order, included my ring size, wrote a check, and mailed it to Sears. The ring came in the mail when Bill wasn't there, but I didn't open it. I wanted to, but I waited.

When Bill came to visit and opened the package, the ring was more beautiful than I could have imagined. It was a few days before my birthday, but smiling, Bill proposed to me again. And I accepted. He slipped the ring on my finger.

He added the wedding ring on May 14, the day we were married.

I wore the rings for many decades, never wanting any other. Eventually, the rings became so worn the diamond was in danger of falling out. Bill bought me a new ring. I had the old rings melted and molded into an ornate pendant with the diamond mounted in it. I wore the pendant on a chain and eventually gave it to a granddaughter.

At that time, not many women got an engagement ring, only a simple gold band, if anything. How could I have known then how blessed I was and would be for having Bill as my soulmate for fifty- eight years before he passed. We will be together again someday.

YOU'RE PERFECT
JUST LIKE YOU ARE

On the evening of New Year's Day, 2007, Bill and I were reclining and relaxing together on our settee. We were ~~and~~ watching TV and snacking on goodies left from the Christmas holidays.

We just had a wonderful family Christmas season. After our usual feast on Christmas Eve Day, a friend of mine who played Santa visited in our home as he had for years. He handed out the gifts I had set out on the porch for him to give to the little kids. We got excited and rowdy, especially Santa. He sang Christmas songs with us and read "The Night Before Christmas."

Between Christmas and New Year's Day, Bill and I went to Missouri to visit my brothers and their families, more great holiday food, and treats. So, on New Year's Day evening, Bill and I were content to settle onto the settee alone together back home. We were feeling well-fed, maybe overfed, and still snacking.

Over the last few years, I had become more health-conscious. Maybe vanity entered into it, too, because of not being able to get into some of my favorite clothes. I had lost a couple of dress sizes. I still needed to lose a few more pounds, including those I had gained during the holidays. I was determined to continue the progress.

As we were snacking, I said to Bill, "I've got to get back to losing weight, especially those I just gained."

He said nothing, and I wasn't sure he heard me. After a moment, though, he said, in a soft, quiet voice, "Nah, you're perfect just like you are."

I was speechless. Really, I was, and taken aback but, oh, so pleased. No compliment could top that, even if it weren't true.

Bill's health was fragile. When that happened in the past, they adjusted his treatments, and his health improved. But, fragile health didn't stop him from living life to the fullest. In late fall, Bill had bargained for and bought, on a handshake, a small used motor home for our usual trips to the Ozarks in the spring.

On January 2nd, he paid for it in full from savings and drove it home. We stocked it with supplies, turned on the furnace, and enjoyed sitting in the camper, even though it was snowing and cold outside. We sometimes ate meals, watched TV, but chose not to sleep in it overnight. And we made plans for our trips when the weather was warmer.

Within a few days, though, Bill went to the hospital for a blood transfusion and tests. In a few days, they sent him home on Hospice. That day, on January 11th, he was called home to Heaven.

I met Bill when I was sixteen. After dating for two years, when I was eighteen, we married. We were married for almost 58 years. After all these years, I still miss him as much as ever.

Bill's compliment is one of my most wonderful and treasured memories of him, even though it may not have been true. But, hopefully, maybe he thought so. Or maybe he wanted to tell me he thought so. When I see Bill in Heaven, he won't have to exaggerate.

While I would still like to lose some weight, I know when I see Bill in Heaven, I will hear his soft voice saying, "You're perfect just like you are."

DEAR BILL...

Each year when Valentine's Day draws near, my mind goes back to remembering the many valentines my Bill and I shared in our many years of marriage, and the two years we dated. We met when I was sixteen, and we married when I was eighteen.

I soon learned that Bill loved giving and receiving greeting cards for holidays and special occasions—especially valentines. He saved all the cards our four kids, and I gave him in the secretary desk that I gave him a few years after we were married to keep his papers, bills, and keepsakes organized and in order.

When we had been married several years, we had an especially difficult winter. The weather was extremely severe, and the bills were high. We had a skimpy Christmas. The kids didn't seem to notice, but Bill and I did. Also, there were many sicknesses: tonsillectomies, appendectomies, and colds, to name a few. Because of all the problems, we didn't agree on much, often arguing or not speaking at all. I knew, however, that I loved him, and he loved me.

As Valentine's Day approached, as always, I looked for a valentine for him. But they all seemed so glossy and phony, at least I thought Bill would think they were. So, one day while he was at work, I took a half sheet of white paper and a red ink pen and wrote a note in longhand in non-rhyming poetry form. I titled it "Dear Bill, I Love You," stating how he was a good husband, a good father, always there for us, and other qualities he demonstrated.

On Valentine's Day, Bill was home for lunch, sitting quietly in his captain's chair, watching TV. The kids were at school. I laid the folded note I had written on the table beside his plate. He ate lunch, then left to go back to work. I didn't see him read the note. He didn't comment on it, but it disappeared.

Later that afternoon, when he came home from work, he brought me the usual—or unusual—large, fancy, valentine-shaped box of expensive chocolates. He never said so, but I believe the reason he could afford such a large, expensive box of chocolates was that they were greatly discounted late on Valentine's Day. It didn't matter to me, because he, the kids, and I had all the candy we wanted.

A few days later, while looking in his desk for something, I saw the note I had written among his keepsakes.

With the coming of spring, we began working through our problems. We started appreciating and enjoying each other's company. I often noticed the note I wrote in his desk, but neither of us ever mentioned it.

Over time, the continuing struggles, stresses, and disappointments in life again caused frictions.

Then one day, when I was at home alone at his desk, looking over the bills, wondering how we would pay them, I noticed the note I wrote again. On an impulse, I jerked it out of the slot and ripped it into several pieces.

Bill never mentioned the missing note. I never mentioned it, but I'm sure he noticed.

Well, we finally grew up and became better at communicating and working through our problems. The whole family took many vacations, especially to Colorado. It didn't hurt that my brother had a horse ranch there. We also went to the Ozarks in Missouri, where Bill's parents lived.

Throughout this time, there were many boxes of candy, and many valentines exchanged. One valentine, in particular, stands out, and I still have it. It reads: *I'm so glad that in God's design, He planned it so your path crossed mine.*

I often thought of rewriting the note, expanding a little on it. After many years I did but wasn't sure how or when to give it to him. Then the right time came! The small church Bill and I attended planned a Valentine Banquet for all the couples at a nearby restaurant in the banquet room.

At the same time, we had a women's Bible Study group that was discussing marriage relationships. I told them about the note and its history and about not giving the rewritten version to Bill. I read it to them. They liked it, and someone suggested that I read it to him at the couple's banquet. All agreed to keep it a secret, and the pastor agreed to go along with the plan and help us.

After the banquet meal, and while everyone was still sitting, the pastor stood and said, "Bonnie has something to share with us."

I stood up behind Bill, who was still seated, and read the newly written note. "Dear Bill…."

Bill sat quietly, as did all the others, for a long moment. Then the men started coming over to him, where he was still seated. They shook his hand, smiled, and said he was making it hard for them to live up to him. I was so proud of him. I noticed his dimples deepen, which meant he was smiling on the inside.

After saying our goodbyes to all our friends in the banquet room, Bill helped me into my winter coat. Then we slipped out into the winter night, but the cold didn't bother us. The snow softly fell as we headed for home to enjoy the rest of the evening together.

Bill has been waiting for me in Heaven for over ten years. When the time comes, we will spend Eternity together, talking, and agreeing on everything. Well, almost everything.

All of my early childhood dreams have come true. They included:

- Marry a good-looking man and have good-looking children. I did, and they were!
- Have two boys and two girls. I did.
- Be a nurse. I am.
- Fly an airplane. I did!

An Old Country Girl's Beginning

Bonnie Lacey Krenning

Made in the USA
Coppell, TX
09 November 2023

23965652R00125